cocktails by flavor

cocktails
by flavor

over 340
recipes to tempt the taste buds

salvatore calabrese

STERLING

New York / London
www.sterlingpublishing.com

Deep Thinker is a cocktail made with cilantro leaves and **Breakfast Martini** is made with medium-cut orange marmalade.

To my dear wife, Sue, and my family: thanks again for your support.

Created by Lynn Bryan,
The BookMaker, London
Design by Mary Staples
Photography by Ian O'Leary

STERLING and the distinctive Sterling logo are registered trademarks of Sterling Publishing Co., Inc.

Library of Congress Cataloging-in-Publication Data Available

Calabrese, Salvatore.
  Cocktails by flavor : over 340 recipes to tempt the taste buds / Salvatore Calabrese.
     p. cm.
  Includes index.
  ISBN-13: 978-1-4027-5305-3
  ISBN-10: 1-4027-5305-5
  1. Cocktails. 2. Bartending. I. Title.
TX951.C25265 2008
641.8'74--dc22   2007045163

10 9 8 7 6 5 4 3 2 1

Published by Sterling Publishing Co., Inc.
387 Park Avenue South,
New York, NY 10016
© 2008 by Salvatore Calabrese
Distributed in Canada by Sterling Publishing
c/o Canadian Manda Group, 165 Dufferin Street,
Toronto, Ontario, Canada M6K 3H6
Distributed in the United Kingdom by GMC Distribution Services,
Castle Place, 166 High Street, Lewes, East Sussex, England BN7 1XU
Distributed in Australia by Capricorn Link (Australia) Pty. Ltd.
P.O. Box 704, Windsor, NSW 2756, Australia

Printed in China
All rights reserved

Sterling ISBN-13: 978-1-4027-5305-3
       ISBN-10: 1-4027-5305-5

For information about custom editions, special sales, premium and corporate purchases, please contact Sterling Special Sales Department at 800-805-5489 or specialsales@sterlingpublishing.com.

contents

introduction   8

getting it right   12
bartender's tools   16
selecting your glassware   18
preparing cocktails   20
storing spirits & wine   19
garnishes   24
useful information   30
measurements   32
bar terms   33

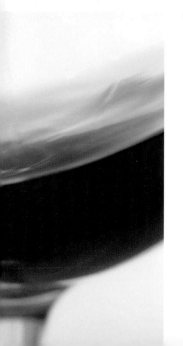

true spirits   34
base flavors for cocktails   36
brandy   38
gin   42
rum   44
tequila   46
vodka   48
scotch & whiskey   50
sake   52

a to z of flavors   54

bitters   56
fruits   64
herbs   130
nut flavors   144
spices   150
sweet & creamy   160
unusual flavors   168
vegetables   174
wine flavors   184

index   192

acknowledgments   222

introduction

On Italy's Amalfi Coast there is one flavor above all others that hangs in the air, day and night: the flavor of lemon. This is because the daredevil drive coast to my home town of Maiori is where the world-famous limoncello liqueur is produced. Lemon groves line the roads, set on tiers of teetering ledges that cascade down the mountainside. Tree branches are laden with lemons, their skins ripening from pale to dark in the warmth of a Mediterranean sun.

From childhood to adulthood, a sense of flavor filled my life. So when my publisher suggested writing a book on cocktails by flavor, I was immediately taken back to those citrus-flavored early years.

I learned about flavor from Raffaello, the bartender who taught me nearly everything I knew about the bar business back then. In our quiet moments, he would mix a cocktail, ask me to blind taste it, then tell him the flavors that were in it. We would do this time and time again as I learned how to detect the bitter taste of Campari, a light Scotch whisky, brandy in a Sidecar, and the Brandy Alexander with its creamy finish. I grew up with the classics, which remain among my favorite cocktails to this day.

Sip by sip I savored the flavors that filled my mouth, setting off taste buds that had lain dormant until the very second that aged rum or fine Scotch malt whisky whacked against their sensory nodules. "Wow!" and "Wow!" again echoed in my mind as my taste memory worked overtime to file away these sensations.

Throughout my career, there has been a certainty: one flavor is not more popular than another. Certainly, flavors come and go with trends because drinkers like to follow the fashion and like to

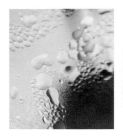

drink what's IN right now. Classicists rarely stray from the tried-and-true that they look forward to, such as a Martini or a Manhattan, because the taste of a cocktail is why you drink it. You do not usually choose a cocktail because of its fancy name, or the incredibly cool, stylish glass in which it is served.

For decades, the number one spirit of choice has been vodka, straight and pure and, ironically, tasteless. However, this lack of flavor has made it perfect as a spirit base. You can combine anything with it. Gin has always had a unique flavor, due to the combinations of botanicals in it. But vodka is the preferable base for building upon. Take the Cosmopolitan—would cranberry and lime juices and Cointreau taste the same with rum? No.

These days, vodka distillers manufacture ranges of triple- and quadruple-distilled, and triple-filtered, vodkas to convince drinkers that vodka can have a true spirit flavor. And, vodkas are also produced in a wide range of intoxicating flavors, including cherry, vanilla, rose, pepper, raspberry, peach, grapefruit, black currant, mandarin, mango, orange, horseradish, lemon, and pear.

Rum has been flavored with coconut for some decades, and now tequila producers are flavoring a few of their exquisite tequilas. Exotic liqueurs now join the familiar sweet liqueurs and cordials on the shelf to add another taste level. Juice manufacturers explore new flavors such as pomegranate and juice from the acai berry, which leads me to the other factor in this current explosion of flavors. A sense of "How healthy is what I'm putting in my body?" reigns. People want the thrill of alcohol but they are also health-conscious.

It is a stirring time to be a bartender. The trend for infusions offers a wealth of flavors that can be made following an age-old, do-it-yourself tradition of merging spirit and flavor. Herbs such as lavender and rosemary, spices such as chili and saffron, and vegetables such as cucumber offer opportunities for cocktail recipes.

This book is divided into three sections. The first is called "Getting It Right" and contains the basics of bar equipment, glassware, preparing a cocktail, how to store spirits and wine, how to make a garnish, advice on ice, a list of terms you might come across in the recipes, and spirit measurements.

The second section is called "True Spirits" and examines the flavors of brandy, gin, rum, tequila, Scotch, whiskey, and sake. The third section is also interesting: An "A to Z of Flavors," within which recipes are presented under Bitters, Fruits, Herbs, Nut Flavors, Spices, Sweet & Creamy, Unusual, Vegetables, and Wine Flavors.

Finally, experimenting with flavors is essential to the development of a successful cocktail list. I'd like to thank FIFTY St James for their support and my team at Salvatore at FIFTY for their inspiration. We had fun creating the recipes and I hope you, too, enjoy making these intriguing cocktails.

However, to me, no other flavor surpasses a cocktail glass filled with vodka straight from the freezer, a whiff of vermouth, and the teardrops of a twist of lemon. My Martini!

Salvatore Calabrese

GETTING IT

mix shake tools flavors muddle spiral
bitter glassware twist muddle garnish
blend shake layer mix shake tools
flavor muddle blend spiral
garnish layer mix shake tools flavors

right

muddle **blend** spiral garnish **twist**

flavors muddle spiral garnish

tools mix shake **tools** flavors **muddle**

blend spiral **garnish** layer mix **shake** terms

flavors blend **muddle** blend

what flavor is that?

Flavor

Now there's a word to start the taste buds watering. Strictly defined, the word flavor is about "the blend of taste and smell sensations evoked by a substance in the mouth." Every bartender will agree with that definition. Each cocktail he or she makes is a blend of aromatic sensations, with every sip a palate pleaser.

Here's the science . . .

for those who like things proven. Recent research has confirmed that bitter, along with sweet, salty, sharp (sour), and spicy are the only tastes that humans can detect. Taste buds, little organs located all over the tongue, interpret or pick up the sense of which flavors are in food and drink. All other flavors are experienced primarily through aroma. Also, it's been confirmed that an affinity for sweet and an aversion to bitter flavors are part of our genetic makeup.

sweet

Examples of cocktails in this category:
Banana Daiquiri
Sweet Sue
Peach Schnapps

sharp (sour)

Examples of cocktails in this category:
Whiskey Sour
Margarita
Lemon Drop

bitter

Examples of cocktails in this category:
Campari Nobile
Negroni
Apothecary Cocktail

salty

Examples of cocktails in this category:
Dirty Martini
Salty Dog
Tequila shot

spicy

Examples of cocktails in this category:
Bloody Mary
Arabian Dream
Spicy Fifty

Earthy is a description I like to use when talking about brandy and whiskey. There are lots of combinations of the five, such as sweet/sour, bitter/salty, sour/salty, bitter/sweet, sweet/sour/spicy, sour/spicy, and bitter/sour, etc.

Development of your palate is the key to discovering one flavor among all others. By refining your palate, you learn which flavors you like and dislike and build up a "flavor memory bank." I recommend you move one ingredient at a time all over the mouth so you can register its flavor. Then you can "search" for it when it is layered with others.

Basically, a cocktail consists of the spirit base, the modifier (aromatizer), and the coloring agent, or special flavoring. In exotic cocktails there may be more than one flavoring agent and some recipes have club soda, ginger ale, or sparkling water as a special effervescent effect.

Modifiers are the calming elements and include vermouths, wine, fruit juices, cream, eggs, and sugar.

The coloring agent, or special flavoring category, includes fruit syrups such as grenadine or orgeat, and other liqueurs and cordials. It is important that any of the additions do not overwhelm the flavor of the base spirit but allow it to come through in the finished cocktail.

the recipe is placed in one category. It is because of all the reasons I have talked about here. In a Mai Tai, for instance, it is the flavor of the orgeat that lingers in the mouth. In a Dirty Martini, it is the olive flavor that remains, with the strength of the vodka. The cocktails have been placed in the category of the one last, lingering flavor that dominates on the finish.

The section that begins on page 34 presents true spirit flavors—brandy, gin, rum, tequila, vodka, whisky, and sake, which is more a rice wine than a spirit, but I have included it here.

In the various sections, you might be surprised to discover some new and exotic flavors that offer an unusual experience for your palate such as lush pomegranate juice, full of antioxidants, or a horseradish vodka flavor, and a recipe using acai berry juice. There is even a category of cocktails made with beet juice! The recipes begin with Bitters, Fruits, Herbs, Nut flavors, Spices, Sweet & Creamy, Unusual flavors, and end with a selection of Wine-flavored cocktails, including champagne.

Some flavors are simple and true, such as strawberry, while others can be a combination of several fruits, vegetables, herbs, and spirits, which together create a new and distinct flavor.

You may wonder why, when you look at a recipe with several fruit juices in it,

A piece of advice: Follow the ingredients to the last drop and your cocktail will turn out fine. Enjoy!

bartender's tools

Certain tools and equipment can help you make delicious cocktails. Following is a list of my favorites. The items on this list are readily available at most houseware stores.

Bar knife
A small, sharp knife used for slicing fruit.

Barspoon
It has a small bowl at the end of a handle.

Blender
Use to combine spirits, juice, fruit, and ice.

Bottle opener
Choose a strong opener that feels good in your hand.

Champagne stopper
Useful for keeping the bubbles in a bottle.

Chopping board
Use to slice fruit for garnishes.

Cocktail sticks
Use for spearing pieces of fruit and cherries for garnishes.

Corkscrew
Use to open wine bottles.

Dash pourer
Use for drops and dashes of bitters and some liqueurs when floating them.

Ice bucket and tongs
Essential for making chilled drinks. Use the tongs.

Ice scoop
Use to add ice to a shaker or blender.

Juicer
Important for making fresh orange, lemon, and lime juices.

Mini grater
Use to dust a drink with chocolate or nutmeg.

Mixing glass
Used for mixing two or more ingredients with a barspoon.

Muddler
Use to mash sprigs of mint or berries into a pulp in the bottom of a mixing glass, shaker, or old-fashioned glass.

Pony jigger
Use for correct measures to balance the flavor and strength of a cocktail.

Salt and pepper grinders
Use to provide a spicy flavor in cocktails, e.g., the Bloody Mary.

Shaker
Use for combining various spirits and juice together with ice.

Stirrers
Stirrers can be made of glass or silver.

Strawberry huller
Use to take the stem and hull from a strawberry.

Straws
Use short straws for a small glass; for highball and goblets, use two longer straws. Plain straws are best.

Zester
Use on lemon, orange, and lime peels to make garnishes.

Boston shaker

regular shaker

mixing glass,
barspoon,
strainer

muddler

bitters bottle

pony jigger

small bottle

tray

champagne
cork

tongs

bottle opener

spirits
pourer

selecting your glassware

In my experience, fine, clear glasses reveal a cocktail in all its beauty. Traditionally, each type of drink has a glass shape specifically for it. For instance, a long drink needs a highball; a Martini is served in a Martini/cocktail glass, a Margarita is at home in a Margarita glass, and a straight shot requires a shot glass.

When buying stemmed glasses, seek out those with a design on the stem. It adds a visual interest to the presentation. Avoid any type of glass with a colored bowl. This hides the color of a cocktail.

Always handle a stemmed glass by the stem, not the bowl. This helps keep the cocktail chilled. And, keep a clean dish towel nearby to polish glasses, thus removing any trace of dishwashing liquid.

Main Glass Types and Sizes

Cocktail:	4oz (12cl)
Old-fashioned:	5 to 6oz (15 to 18cl)
Shot:	2 to 3oz (6 to 9cl)
Liqueur:	2 to 3oz (6 to 9cl)
Highball:	10oz (30cl)
Wine:	4 to 9oz (12 to 27cl)

There are many glass styles. However, you need only a basic selection. The cocktail glass is by far the most popular shape for almost any cocktail served without ice. A flute is essential for champagne cocktails, and an old-fashioned glass is good for short drinks. The highball is king of the long drink glasses.

In the recipe section, a small icon of the recommended glass shape has been placed at the start of the ingredients as a useful guide.

champagne flute
A flute's shape brings the bubbles to the surface.

champagne coupe
A small glass used for serving after-dinner digestifs.

cocktail
A regular-sized cocktail glass is best for these recipes.

cognac
The balloon shape of a glass for cognac.

goblet
This is best for exotic cocktails with lots of color and a few juices.

highball
Used for long drinks. Also known as a tumbler.

hot toddy/irish coffee
Designed to withstand the heat of coffee.

margarita
A glass for Margaritas.

old-fashioned
A short glass with a heavy base so it sits in the palm of your hand.

piña colada
The glass style for the famous Piña Colada cocktail.

shot
Designed for a measure of a strong spirit that is downed in one gulp.

white and red wine
Wine glasses are good for cocktails that include mixers and juices and a fancy garnish. Sizes range from 4oz/12cl to 6oz/18cl for white and from 6 oz/18cl to 9oz/27cl for red.

storing spirits & wine

storing & serving champagne

Champagne should ideally be kept in a rack in a horizontal position. Try to maintain a consistent temperature. A warning: Do not freeze a champagne bottle to chill it quickly. This can ruin the contents. Always use clean champagne flutes which have been wiped of any trace of residual dishwashing liquid.

opening champagne

Wrap a clean towel around the bottle and hold it firmly in one hand. With the other, undo the wire around the cork. Point the top away from you and any guests and gently push the cork with both thumbs to release it. Turn the bottle as you do this.

When pouring champagne, aim for the middle of the flute and pour slowly. Pause after a few moments to let the bubbles subside, then start pouring again. Fill to only three-quarters full.

storing wine

Store red wine at room temperature. Do not place a bottle of claret or burgundy in the refrigerator. It is best to store a bottle on its side, so that any sediment can fall to the bottom when you stand it upright.

White wines are best kept chilled. It is best not to place bottles in the freezer to chill since this has a detrimental effect.

storing spirits & eaux-de-vie in the freezer

When you place a bottle of spirit such as gin, vodka, aquavit, Poire William, kirsch, framboises, and kümmel in the freezer you will discover it does not freeze. This is because the spirit is 80 percent proof (40 percent alcohol by volume). Be careful not to put a bottle containing a spirit lower than that measurement, say, 74 percent proof (37 percent abv), because the spirit will freeze and the bottle may even crack. Chilling a spirit helps the cocktail remain cold while you drink it.

chilling a cocktail glass

Rule number one: Always chill a cocktail glass before you pour any liquid into it. The chilled effect makes a drink look fabulous and appealing.

Put the required number of glasses in the freezer for a few hours before you need to use them. Or, fill them with crushed ice—this will chill the glass in advance of the cocktail being poured in. Tip this ice away before adding the drink.

preparing cocktails

using a shaker

A recipe that contains spirits, juice, and light cream can be shaken. The most common two shakers are the Boston shaker and the two-piece metal shaker. The Boston shaker is made of two pieces—one is metal, the other is clear glass. The ingredients are poured in the glass section so you can see what you are doing, then ice is added. The metal part covers the glass, and is sealed with a gentle slap of the palm.

Turn the shaker upside down. When the drink is shaken, the liquid will end up in the metal part. Let the drink settle for a moment before parting the two sections. If you can't open it easily, place your thumb under the center section, where the metal and glass meet, and push gently. This will break the air vacuum inside.

To serve the drink, pour it through a bar strainer, holding it firmly over the shaker's opening.

The regular shaker consists of a base, a small section with a fitted strainer, and a lid. It's usually compact, small, and easy to handle. Always be sure you hold the lid down firmly. If it gets stuck, ease the lid up with both thumbs. Sometimes a quick, hard twist will do the trick.

Also, if you have shaken it for a while, wipe the outside down with a cloth. This warms the sides and loosens the vacuum.

how to muddle

To muddle you need a muddler. Sometimes, the end of a barspoon has a muddler attached. More bartenders are using this method today—instead of bashing the fruits to a pulp, as when using a blender, this brings out the essence, and the freshness of the fruit remains intact.

Mostly, fruits or mint are muddled directly in the base of the glass, or in a shaker. Choose a glass with a heavy base. Dice the fruit and place in the glass or shaker. Add sugar (if stated) and/or a dash of spirit or wine (if stated) and push down on the fruit until the juice oozes out.

This photograph was taken after about one minute of muddling diced limes. You can see how much juice can be released through constant pressure.

using a mixing glass

Cocktails whose ingredients mix easily and must be served chilled are made (built) directly into a mixing glass, then poured into a glass. Always place about six ice cubes into the mixing glass first and, using a barspoon, stir the ice around to chill the glass. Strain off any excess water. Add each spirit and stir the mixture well. Strain using a bar strainer into the glass. Classic cocktails such as the Negroni and the Manhattan are always stirred in a mixing glass.

Note how much ice has been put in the mixing glass and how the spirit passes over the ice cubes. It gets chilled on the way.

creating a layered drink

The answer to layering is in the weight of each spirit in the recipe.

Generally, layered drinks are made in shot or liqueur glasses. All you need is a steady hand and a barspoon. Then you float one liquid over the previous one.

Read the label on the spirit or liqueur bottle to discover the alcohol volume—the lower it is, the more sugar it contains, and it will be heavier, like a syrup. If there are five ingredients in a recipe, such as in a Pousse-Café, begin with the first liquid ingredient in the recipe—the heaviest. To pour the second, less heavy ingredient, pick up the barspoon and place it in the glass on the edge of the first layer, with the back of the barspoon facing up.

Pour the next amount slowly onto the highest point of the spoon, and it will gradually flow down to create a second layer. Repeat the action for each of the successive lighter layers.

Place the barspoon well under the ice cubes and stir to combine the spirits.

Pour slowly from a height, being careful not to splash over the edge of the glass.

blending cocktails

As a general rule, you blend any recipe that contains cream, fruit, and crushed ice. How much to make? Usually a recipe is for one drink, but for the blender it is sometimes best to make two or more drinks at one time, especially if you are making the cocktails during a party.

Always wash, peel, and dice the fruit before adding it to the blender. And make sure there is enough liquid in the blender, too. You may have to add a dash of white wine or spirit to make it easier to blend.

Some blended recipes require the mixture to be also strained through a sieve, making a liquid with a finer texture. This is easy to do: place the sieve over the glass and pour small amounts of the mixture into the sieve. With a teaspoon or barspoon, mash the mixture until you can see that most of the liquid has passed through the holes in the wire mesh. Then discard the remaining pits or flesh and pour in a further small amount, repeating the process.

Blended cocktails are best served immediately. You can blend the fruits and spirit before an event, and place in the refrigerator, but do not add creamy ingredients until the last minute. Add the ice at the final moment.

garnishes

Garnishes are the finishing touch. Firstly, consider the flavor of the cocktail you are making. Match the garnish with the dominating flavor. Secondly, consider the color of the garnish. Select something that will look as if it belongs to the drink. Thirdly, a garnish must be in proportion to the size of the glass and not look as if it is an afterthought.

Strawberries can be dropped in the drink, particularly into a flute, or perched on the rim. To make a strawberry fan, take out the green stem, and slice into as many pieces as you want without separating them. Fan out the slices and slip the strawberry over the rim. Or use a whole hulled strawberry, make a small slit in the bottom, and slip it over the rim.

frost/crust the rim of a glass

Classic cocktails such as a Margarita and a Daiquiri require a frosted (or crusted) rim. To achieve the look, rub a wedge of lime around the rim and then dip the rim of the glass in fine sea salt.

If a sugar-frost rim is required, pour some superfine (caster) sugar in a saucer, rub the rim with a wedge of lemon, orange, or lime (whatever the recipe calls for), and dip the rim in the sugar.

Cut a slit in the wedge of lemon and insert the wedge over the rim of the cocktail glass.

Make sure the sugar (or salt) is on both sides of the rim, and that there is enough of the substance to remain on the glass when you shake it.

make an apple fan

Cut a small green apple in half. Using a sharp knife, cut one half into vertical slices. Take five of these in your hand and fan them out like a pack of cards. Pierce the base of the fan with a toothpick.

make a slice

Take a fresh washed and dried lime and place it on the cutting board. Hold it firmly with the tip of your fingers. With the knife, slice firmly through the skin and flesh to make a slender slice. Use the slices cut from the middle of the lime.

make a wedge

Cut a fresh lime in half vertically. Place it flesh down on the cutting board. With a sharp knife, cut into the lower side of the lime and slice a wedge. Repeat the action until the entire half-lime is in several small wedges.

make a spiral

Using a zester, starting from the top, cut around an orange, making a long spiral. Hold the fruit in your hand and press the zester firmly into the peel. Work slowly until you have a long and winding spiral. Take a swizzle stick and wrap the spiral around it tightly. When you reach the end of the spiral gently roll it off the swizzle stick. Place it in the drink, with a little bit of it hanging over the rim.

1 As you push down with the zester into the skin, turn the orange around as you are doing it. This helps you see if you are keeping in a straight line, or going in the wrong direction.

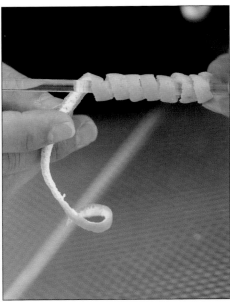

2 Hold the swizzle stick in one hand and start to wrap the orange peel around it from the end nearest the hand that holds it. Twist the peel with the free hand, keeping it tightly wound around the stick.

3 Here you can see the final spiral in the drink and hanging loosely over the rim of the glass. Check the proportion of the spiral—it does not need to be too long or it will look like a piece of Christmas ribbon.

make a twist

A twist of lemon, lime, or orange is the type of garnish you will use for many of the classic cocktails, as well as some of the newer-style Martinis.

The secret of the twist is in its ability to add the fruit's essence to a cocktail without drowning the other flavors in the drink. A hint is more interesting than a wallop! When twisting the peel you can see the drops of essence that fall into the drink. It is also a way to add flair to your method of making a drink. A stylish finishing touch is always welcome.

You will see a bartender squeeze a twist of lemon into a classic gin or vodka Martini, the champagne cocktail Alfonso, a classic Rusty Nail, and the Sazerac. In many cases, the bartender will twist and then drop the peel into the glass.

The twist has a second role to play in the making of a cocktail. Sometimes, a bartender will add a little hint of flavor by wiping the twist around the rim. When you pick up the glass, the aroma of the fruit is right on the nose.

1 Hold the fruit upright as shown. With a sharp knife, cut a reasonably wide section from the side of a fresh and clean lemon, orange, or lime.

4 Hold the twist over the drink with your fingertips (as shown) and squeeze it to release the teardrops of essence.

2 Place the section on the cutting board and trim each side neatly.

3 Turn the piece of rind over, and gently cut off the pith. Discard the pith.

5 You can also run the twist around the rim of the glass, using the pith side. This is a quick movement right around the rim, then you can drop it in the cocktail.

useful information

how to make a syrup

Many recipes call for gomme syrup, but you can make your own sugar syrup using granulated sugar. Gradually stir 4 cups (100cl) of granulated sugar into 2 cups (50cl) of boiling water in a saucepan. Bring it to a boil and simmer. Skim it, allow to cool, and pour into small, clean bottles. Store in a dark cupboard.

To make a flavored syrup, such as thyme, bring 2 cups (50cl) of water to a boil. Add a large handful of fresh thyme. Boil for five minutes. Add 4 cups (100cl) of sugar, stir, then simmer until the sugar dissolves. Remove the mixture from the heat. Store as above.

a note about egg white

Combining egg white with the other ingredients then shaking gives a drink a white frothy head. If you are concerned about using fresh egg white, then use egg white powder instead.

juicing limes

When choosing a lime, the freshest one will have a paler green skin. If it's rind is dark green, you will get less juice from it. Some bartenders roll a lime prior to juicing. The rolling action separates the juice from the pith inside the lime. You can also put the lime in hot water for about 30 seconds. This action releases the juice inside. Then cut the skin with a sharp fruit knife.

Just squeezing the fruit is not enough to get the juice out. Use a hand juicer—it also stops the seeds (if there are any) from escaping into the drink.

ice

Ice must be fresh and dry. Use filtered or bottled water to make ice. Ice should taste only of water.

Why do you need ice? Ice is used to cool spirits as they are poured into a glass. Ice is available crushed, shaved, cracked, or cubed. Cracked and shaved ice are more watery than dry ice cubes. When added to a drink, the spirit is more immediately diluted. With solid ice cubes, the ice holds its water for longer through the sipping. The average ice cube contains between 1 and $1^1/2$oz (3 to 4.5cl) water but the water melts very slowly.

As a general rule, ice cubes are used for cocktails made in a shaker. Crushed ice is used for drinks created in a blender. The crushed ice is used only in the blender, not in the glass, unless the recipe specifically states "Use crushed ice." Ice cubes are used in old-fashioned glasses and highballs, and never in a cocktail glass unless you are using ice to chill it before pouring in the drink.

Remember, do not use any of the ice remaining in a shaker for the next drink because the ice will be broken and will retain the flavor of the previous drink. And we can't have that!

In **Va-Va-Voom** you can see how much crushed ice you need to add to a highball.

measurements

It is best to use a double-ended pony jigger when making cocktails because it helps you measure the specific amount of spirit, liqueur, or juice stated in a recipe.

One of its cups measures 1oz, the other 2oz. Some types have smaller $^1/_4$ and $^1/_2$oz measurements marked inside the 2oz end.

The recipes in this book are given in ounces for American readers, and also in centiliters for readers familiar with metric measurements.

The recipes in this guide are based on:

$^1/_3$oz = 1cl
$^2/_3$oz = 2cl
$^1/_2$oz = 1.5cl
Therefore 1oz = 3cl, 2oz = 6cl, etc.

At first, it is a good idea to use the jigger for exact amounts so you gain a good idea of what the cocktails should taste like. As your confidence grows, you might add more of this and a dash of that to change the taste to satisfy your palate.

The thing to remember is: Be consistent and retain the proportions.

• The standard size of a cocktail is 3oz/15cl.

• Tall drinks like highballs contain no more than 8oz/24cl.

• Medium-sized cocktails are about 5oz/15cl.

• A spirit served on the rocks measures about 1$^1/_2$oz/4.5cl.

• Wine glasses usually hold from about 4 to 5oz/12 to 15cl.

• A glass is always filled to about a level of three-quarters, never all the way.

how many drinks can you get from one bottle?

If a bottle contains 23oz (approximately 75cl) and a cocktail recipe calls for 1$^2/_3$oz/5cl, for example, then you can make 14 of that particular cocktail.

bar terms

Following is a list of terms that you may come across.

Aperitif
A cocktail served before dinner to stimulate the appetite.

Barspoon
A long-handled spoon used for mixing spirits and liqueurs in a mixing glass.

Blend
To use an electric blender to make a smooth liquid from fruit, juice, coconut cream, or cream.

Brut
Dry (when referring to champagne).

Build
To pour the ingredients directly into a mixing or serving glass.

Dash
A small amount that flows when a bottle is quickly inverted once.

Digestif
A cocktail served after dinner to aid digestion.

Float
To float one spirit or liqueur over another.

Frosted glass
A glass that's been chilled in the freezer.

Frosted/crusted rim
A glass with has a salted or sugared rim.

Mixing glass
A large professional glass with measurements marked on the side.

Muddle
A term meaning to crush with vigor.

Neat
Serving a drink "straight," without any ice, water, or mixer.

On the rocks
A drink served on ice cubes.

Proof
American description of alcohol content. 100 proof is 50 percent alcohol by volume.

Shake
To use a cocktail shaker to combine all the ingredients.

Short drink
Served in an old-fashioned glass.

Stir
To mix ingredients in a mixing glass.

Spiral
A thin rind of orange, lemon, or lime cut in a horizontal direction around the fruit and used as a garnish.

Tall drink
Served in a highball with ice and measuring 8oz/24cl at the most.

Twist
A thin, long strip of peel twisted in the middle and dropped into the drink.

Zest
A strip of lemon or orange peel.

TRUE

brandy gin vodka whiskey
rum whiskey sake brandy gin
vodka tequila rum tequila sake
brandy gin vodka rum brandy

spirits

brandy gin vodka **sake** whiskey
gin **vodka** brandy rum tequila
rum whiskey sake brandy gin
vodka tequila rum tequila sake

base flavors for cocktails

Taking a bottle of chilled **vodka** from the freezer, I looked at the liquid inside the frosted bottle. The texture was oily and entirely colorless. How, I wondered, was I going to write about the flavor of something so innocuous? I managed to bring my vodka "flavor memory bank" to the surface and, as you will see on page 48, there was something to talk about. Brandy, Scotch, and bourbon whiskey, on the other hand, are full of flavors ranging from dark and oakey to fruity. On pages 38 and 50 respectively I elaborate on each.

The lack of a color in **gin** is another deception in the field of flavor. Depending on the brand, gin can dazzle the taste buds in a hundred ways. It's all in the mix of the botanicals, kept secret by the major distillers. Gin does lend its own flavor to a cocktail, hence the success of the classic Gin Martini dating back to the late 19th century when Jerry "The Professor" Thomas mixed his first recipe. Of course, the gin they drank back then is a far, far different gin than that manufactured today. There is a lot more to read about on Page 42.

These liquors, the dark side of spirits, retain their own flavor when mixed with another ingredient, and come through as the underlying, lingering note. This is not the case with a pure vodka, which is mostly the reason for its unassailable position as the leading spirit in the world. Liquor such as **rums** made from sugarcane have an underlying sweetness but, again, the flavors of individual rums are different, depending on the area from which they come. When you open the bottle, is the sound of a merengue or salsa released, as well as dazzling rays of sunshine? Not quite, but some rums do like to cause a fun, flavor sensation. On page 44, you can learn more about this Caribbean flavor.

Tequila is another fascinating true spirit that's fast catching up with rum and vodka sales. Perhaps, and I am summizing, it is the image tequila has had as the kind of liquor to drink quickly to get drunk quickly. Urban legends reinforced that image with tales of tequila shots, lemon, and salt; lick, suck, and swallow was the action. Tequila has grown up alongside the people who drank those shots. More regulations governing the quality of the many tequilas that come out of Mexico have helped the flavor and hence its image. Buy quality tequilas, then you will appreciate the true essence of a nation even more. Turn to Page 46 to embrace the 100% agave spirit.

Sake, a liquor made from rice wine and therefore not a spirit, although I have included it in this section, is gaining affection in both cocktail and restaurant bars. The more we eat Japanese, the more we are turning to Japanese liquors. Sake is graded according to quality, and this brings a wide range of flavors to the mouth, as you can see on page 52.

In the pages that follow you will discover some classics and some new recipes destined to add more layers to your memory palate.

brandy

Brandy is a generic title which encompasses a brandy that's made anywhere in the world from different types of grapes. The most famous brandy is **cognac** from the Charente-Maritime region in France. The grapes used to make cognac are Ugni Blanc, Folle Blanche, and Colombard. All cognacs start out in new oak to mellow the fiery spirit and give them color. Long-term aging is done in seasoned casks that impart less of the oak flavor while the brandy matures. Flavors to look for in a quality cognac include old port wine, coffee, leaf of Havana cigar, woody, earthy, crème brulée, licorice, honey, truffle notes, spicy, hazelnut, oak, and hints of pear.

California brandies are made from grape varieties such as the Thompson Seedless and Flame Tokay, although a few producers use Ugni Blanc, Colombard, and Folle Blanche grapes.

armagnac

Charlie's Nightcap

1¹/₂oz/4.5cl	**armagnac**
¹/₂oz/1.5cl	**pear liqueur**

Stir and strain into a brandy snifter.

D'Artagnan II

2oz/6cl	**armagnac**
¹/₂oz/1.5cl	**Grand Marnier liqueur**
dash	**fresh orange juice**

GARNISH twist of orange

Shake all ingredients with ice. Strain into an old-fashioned glass filled with ice. Add the garnish.

Armagnac is made in Gascony, in the southwest corner of France, using Ugni Blanc, Folle Blanche, and Colombard grapes. Distillation takes place in the alambic Armagnaçais, a column still process that results in brandy with a rustic character and aroma that requires aging in oak to mellow it out. Flavors to look for include dried tropical fruit, brown spices, pepper, toffee, charred nuts, raisins, smoky oak, earth, and dark caramel flavors.

The French region of Normandy is apple country, and the cider made there can be distilled into an apple brandy known as **calvados.** In the United States, apple brandy is known as applejack, while apple brandies that are similar to an eau-de-vie are made in California and Oregon. Look for flavors of musty apples, oak, earth, some honey, and a well-rounded finish.

cognac

Cognac Frappée

2oz/6cl	cognac	
	crushed ice	

 In a balloon glass filled with crushed ice, pour the cognac. Stir. Serve with a straw (optional).

Sazerac

1²/₃oz/5cl	cognac
one	lump of sugar
2 dashes	Peychaud bitters

GARNISH large lemon peel

 Muddle a lump of sugar with a few drops of Peychaud bitters in the bottom of an old-fashioned glass. Add half of cognac with two ice cubes. Stir for at least a minute. Add two more ice cubes and remaining cognac. Stir for one minute, repeat. Be careful not to water the drink too much. Add the garnish.

Sazerac Grande

1oz/3cl	cognac
²/₃oz/2cl	Grand Marnier liqueur
dash	chilled water
¹/₆oz/.5cl	Pernod (or absinthe)
1	sugar cube
2 dashes	Angostura bitters

Muddle a lump of sugar with a few dashes of bitters in the bottom of an old-fashioned glass. Add half the cognac with two ice cubes. Stir for at least a minute. Add two more ice cubes and remaining cognac. Stir for one minute, repeat one more time. Be careful not to water the drink too much. Add more ice then a quick spray of Pernod absinthe on top.

Sidecar

1²/₃oz/5cl	cognac
³/₄oz/2.5cl	Cointreau
¹/₂oz/1.5cl	fresh lemon juice

GARNISH maraschino cherry

Shake ingredients with ice. Strain into a cocktail glass. Add the garnish in the drink.

calvados

AJ II

2oz/6cl	calvados
¹/₂oz/1.5cl	fresh apple juice
dash	gomme syrup

Shake all ingredients with ice. Strain into a chilled cocktail glass.

Calvados Cocktail

2oz/6cl	calvados
¹/₂oz/1.5cl	Cointreau
¹/₂oz/1.5cl	orange juice

Shake all ingredients with ice. Strain into a chilled cocktail glass.

The two classics **Sidecar** and **Old-Fashioned** remain popular because of the balance of flavors.

gin

Gin is a spirit full of character, with a number of botanical ingredients that stimulate and enliven the palate, keeping it fresh and clean.

An array of exotic, luxury gins designed to lure vodka drinkers has hit the top shelf. For example, a triple-distilled, 94 proof, small-batch gin features an impressive complexity. Manufactured with individually distilled, separately stored oils of herbs and botanicals from nine different countries, the ingredients include corianders from North Africa and West Asia, almonds from

Gibson

2²/₃oz/8cl   **gin**
dash   **dry vermouth**

GARNISH white pearl onion

Pour the gin into a mixing glass filled with ice. Add the dry vermouth and stir. Strain into a chilled cocktail glass. Drop the garnish into the drink.

Gin Martini

3oz/9cl   **gin**
1 to 2 drops   **extra dry vermouth**

GARNISH twist of lemon, or a green olive

Pour the gin directly into a chilled cocktail glass. Float 1 to 2 drops of vermouth over the gin. Twist the lemon peel over the drink. Rub the peel around the rim of the glass, then drop it in. (Drop the olive in the glass if you prefer.)

Java, Cassia bark from tropical Africa and China, cubeb berries from Sri Lanka, licorice from the Mediterranean, lemon from Spain, angelica from Europe and Asia, orris from southern Europe, juniper from Italy, and grains of paradise from South Africa. Now, that's some flavor!

Another small-batch gin is four times distilled, and uses only fresh, hand picked, whole-fruit fresh botanicals, including grapefruit, orange, lime, hints of juniper, with notes of soothing chamomile.

At the other end of the market is a handcrafted gin with only a hint of juniper, along with touches of cilantro, lemon, and orange peel. Triple-distilled for a delicate flavor, it delivers a lighter, crisper taste that gin Martini purists appreciate. Plus, there is that cucumber and rose petal British gin for those who like to be different.

When used in a cocktail, the botanicals cut through the sweetness of liqueurs and sugar. However, gin also enhances fruit flavors, in much the same way a squeeze of lemon does, without altering the flavor profiles.

Pink Gin

2oz/6cl	gin
dash	Angostura bitters
	chilled mineral water
	(optional)

 Pour all ingredients into a mixing glass with ice. Stir. Strain into an old-fashioned glass (no ice). Serve the chilled water in a glass on the side.

Sapphire Martini

| 2oz/6cl | gin |
| dash | Parfait Amour |

GARNISH blueberry or violet flower

 Add the gin into a chilled cocktail glass. Drop the Parfait Amour into the drink. This will sit in the bottom of the glass. Add the blueberry on a cocktail stick. If using a flower, sit this carefully on top of the cocktail.

rum

Search through a bar's cocktail list and you'll discover an array of classic, fresh fruit–infused, or muddled cocktails made with a rum base.

Here is a nectar generally made from molasses, a sugarcane by-product. Its origins are in the Caribbean yet rum is distilled wherever sugarcane is grown. Usually aged in oak casks, rums can be aged for between one to 30 years or more. During this process, rum acquires a golden color that changes to a dark brown in time. (Light rum has any color removed during the filter process, which is just before bottling.)

There are several types of rum: light (white), golden, dark, premium aged, spiced, and overproof. To these, add the spirit cachaça, a pure, sugarcane rum made only in Brazil. It is the base of the über-famous Caribbean cocktail, the Caipirinha.

The very dark, rich-tasting **demerara rum from Guyana** is made by adding spices and fruit to the mix. Rums from Haiti and Martinique are made with sugarcane juice and are smoother on the finish.

Rums are a favorite of bartenders because of their easy mixability with tropical fruit and additional flavors. However, the spirit's flavor is interesting and you don't want to bury it by being overzealous with the other flavors. Dark or light, spiced or not, rum goes with cola, coffee, and fruit such as coconut, mango, banana, pineapple, and papaya.

Adjectives used to describe the flavor of rum are simple: sweet, vanilla, almond, floral, and banana. A lingering finish on the palate will have hints of sugarcane and oak.

The latest trend for a flavored spirit has not passed rum by. Watermelon, coconut, lemon, banana, cherry, orange, and vanilla spice flavored are just a few of the flavored rums available. Yo, ho, ho!

Bacardi Classic Cocktail

1²⁄₃oz/5cl	**light rum**
1oz/3cl	**fresh lime juice**
1 tsp	**grenadine**

GARNISH maraschino cherry

Shake all ingredients with ice. Strain into a chilled cocktail glass. Add the cherry on a cocktail stick across the glass.

Bahama Todd

¹⁄₂oz/1.5cl	**light rum**
¹⁄₂oz/1.5cl	**dark rum**
¹⁄₂oz/1.5cl	**spiced rum**
¹⁄₂oz/1.5cl	**coconut rum**
¹⁄₂oz/1.5cl	**151 proof rum**
¹⁄₂oz/1.5cl	**blue curaçao**
5oz/15cl	**pineapple juice**

Add the first four rums to a highball filled with ice. Add the blue curaçao and the pineapple juice. Stir well. Float the 151 proof rum on top.

Black Dog

2oz/6cl	**light rum**
dash	**dry vermouth**

GARNISH black olive

Add ingredients to a mixing glass filled with ice. Stir. Strain into a chilled cocktail glass. Add the olive.

Rum in the Old-Fashioned Way

2oz/6cl	**aged rum**
dash	**Angostura bitters**
	white sugar cube

GARNISH twist of lime, twist of orange

Place the sugar in an old-fashioned glass and soak with the bitters. Add enough rum to cover the cube, then crush the cube with the back of a barspoon. Add the remaining rum and ice. Stir. Add the garnishes in the drink.

tequila

Tequila is distilled from the fermented juice of the blue agave, a succulent plant found all over Mexico. The spirit has progressed from being a simply distilled product to being a refined and sought-after connoisseur's liquor.

The character of a tequila is determined by the strength to which it is distilled, the type of barrel in which it is aged, and for how long it is aged in the oak barrel. This spirit gains its color, aroma, and flavor from the wood. The flavor differs depending on the whether you are drinking a blanco (silver), gold (its color comes from caramel additive), reposado, or añejo (aged) spirit. Whichever type you drink, it will seduce you with its subtle fragrances and traditional dusky aromas.

Añejo (aged) tequilas, made from 100% blue agave, should be smooth, dark, and rich, bourbonlike in color and taste, which is a result of the spirit having been aged in charcoal barrels.

In a blanco (silver) style, you might find lime, citrus, pear with a herbal note, and spiciness balanced with an earthy tone. Sometimes, a hint of vanilla.

Some artisan tequilas have delicate, floral flavors ranging from a hint of eucalyptus and peppermint in a silver, and fruitiness and tobacco in an añejo. **Triple-distilled tequilas** are intense with agave flavor. **Flavored tequilas**, such as Tropiña, Oranjo, and Citrico, are good to use as a base for tropical fruit cocktails.

Classic Tequila Shot

1oz/3cl	gold tequila
pinch	salt
	wedge of lime

 Pour the tequila into a shot glass. Hold the wedge of lime between your finger and thumb. Place the salt at the base of the thumb on the same hand. Quickly, lick the salt, down the tequila, and bite the lime.

Sangrita Shooter

1²/₃oz/5cl	gold tequila
1²/₃oz/5cl	tomato juice
dash	fresh lime juice
twist	ground black pepper

 Pour the tequila into a shot glass. Mix the tomato and lime juices with the black pepper in a second shot glass. Sip each drink alternately.

Tequila Slammer

1²/₃oz/5cl	añejo (aged) tequila
1²/₃oz/5cl	champagne

 Pour the tequila and champagne into a heavy-based old-fashioned glass. Hold a napkin on top of the glass, and slam the glass down on the table or counter top. Drink the cocktail as it fizzes. (Do this carefully, please, so you do not injure yourself.)

Tequil-ini

2oz/6cl	añejo (aged) tequila
¹/₂oz/1.5cl	dry vermouth

GARNISH twist of lime

 Add the ingredients to a mixing glass filled with ice. Stir until cold and frosty. Strain into a chilled cocktail glass. Add the twist.

vodka

The Finnish like to produce what they refer to as naked vodka, with the purity of the glacial spring water being the key to its flavor. Russian and Eastern European vodka producers add to this concept with a variety of products with a flavor resulting from each vodka being triple distilled and then triple filtered. Vodkas are also fruit-flavored: raspberry, black currant, orange, pomegranate, lemon, and strawberry are just a few of the flavors. Others available include buffalo grass, pepper, horseradish, basil, rose, and vanilla. These are all best served over rocks or chilled straight up.

Level Martini

2oz/6cl	**frozen vodka**
¹/₂oz/1.5cl	**dry sherry**
tsp	**caper juice**

GARNISH caper berry

Place ingredients in a mixing glass filled with ice. Stir. Strain into a chilled cocktail glass. Add the garnish in the drink.

Vodka Martini

2oz/6cl	**frozen vodka**
2 dashes	**extra dry vermouth**

GARNISH twist of lemon or green olive

Pour the vodka into a chilled cocktail glass. Float 2 dashes of vermouth over the top. Add the twist of lemon over the drink. Drop an olive in the glass if you prefer.

A **Level Martini** has an interesting, slightly salty taste from the caper berry juice.

scotch & whiskey

The matter of taste in dark spirits such as American whiskey and Scotch is a complicated one, especially when personal preferences are added into the scenario.

Bourbon is whiskey made in America and must be distilled from fermented grain mash comprised of at least 51 percent corn, which is then aged in charred oak barrels. Some say the color, the caramel, smoke, and vanilla flavors, plus the tannic nip in bourbons is there because of the char. Types of bourbons include single barrel, small batch, and special aged. Other flavors include spice, floral accents, light to medium honey, apricots, cloves, charcoal, citrus, hazelnut, malt, nutmeg, oak, pepper, and maple syrup.

There are five categories of Scotch whisky: single malt, single grain, blended malt, blended Scotch, blended grain Scotch. Each blend has up to 40 to 50 different Scotch whiskies selected for their character, flavor, and bouquet. In general terms Scotch whisky on the palate can present soft and malty flavors, zesty oak and warm peat smoke notes, fresh nutmeg and toasted almonds; it can also be faintly salty and fully peated. Claret, peat, dark chocolate, licorice, peach, Caribbean brown sugar, and tangerine are also found in a Scotch.

In a cocktail, dark spirits hold their own strength when other flavors are added. For instance, in a Rusty Nail the earthy flavor is not overcome by the Drambuie liqueur. The Scotch holds its own as a good Scotch should.

bourbon

New Orleans

2oz/6cl	bourbon
3 dashes	Peychaud bitters
2 dashes	orange curaçao

GARNISH orange peel

Stir all ingredients in a mixing glass with ice. Strain into a chilled cocktail glass. Add the garnish.

Old-Fashioned

2oz/6cl	bourbon
1	white sugar cube
dash	Angostura bitters
	club soda

GARNISH twist of orange, maraschino cherry

Place the sugar cube in the base of an old-fashioned glass. Soak with bitters and a dash of soda water. Crush the sugar with the back of a barspoon. Add half of the bourbon and two ice cubes. Stir. Add more ice and the remaining bourbon. Stir. Decorate with half a slice of orange and a cherry. Serve with a stirrer.

scotch

Rusty Nail

2oz/6cl	Scotch
1oz/3cl	Drambuie

GARNISH twist of lemon

Serve in an old-fashioned glass, on the rocks. Add the garnish.

whiskey

Manhattan

1²/3oz/5cl	Canadian Club whisky
²/3oz/2cl	dry vermouth
2 dashes	Angostura bitters

GARNISH maraschino cherry

Pour all the ingredients over ice in a mixing glass and stir. Strain into a chilled cocktail glass. Drop the cherry in the drink.

sake

Sake is fermented from rice, which is a grain, and is referred to as more like a beer than a wine. However, sake is not carbonated and is more like a wine than a beer in flavor. It is not a distilled beverage and is not related to gin, vodka, or light rum in any way, yet it can, and does, replace these clear spirits in some adventurous cocktail recipes.

This exotic liquor can be sipped warm at room temperature, or taken chilled. Most people know its warmth, but in a cocktail with other ingredients, it takes on a different life.

Blue Rain

1²/₃oz/5cl	sake
²/₃oz/2cl	pear liqueur
¹/₃oz/1cl	blue curaçao
¹/₃oz/1cl	fresh lemon juice

GARNISH wedge of pear

Shake all ingredients with ice.
Strain into a chilled cocktail glass.
Sit the pear on the rim of the glass.

Hong Kong

2oz/6cl	sake
2 dashes	Angostura bitters
²/₃oz/2cl	red vermouth
dash	Campari

GARNISH twist of lemon

Shake the bitters, sake, red vermouth, and Campari with ice.
Strain into a chilled cocktail glass.
Add the garnish.

The sweet, unfiltered *nigori* sake is often used for fruity cocktails because of its pale, milky sweet flavor. The fermented rice ingredient is very important for taste. It can provide a hint of pineapple, or coconut, or tropical fruit in general. Filtered dry sakes are poured into stiffer drinks.

If you get the opportunity to taste a sake before you buy, look for balance in the flavors. Nothing should be cloying or pushy in the flavor. A sake can be quite dry or quite sweet and still be in harmony. It if it is dull and sickly sweet or harsh, try another brand. A gentle hint of fruit and a balanced sweetness are good. Some sakes can enliven the palate with a rush of acidity so be wary of these, too. Other sakes spread flavor into every nook and cranny, and are satisfying on every level.

Sparkling Sakepom

1¹/₂oz/4.5cl	sake
1oz/3cl	pomegranate juice
dash	grenadine
	champagne

Crust a chilled cocktail glass with a mixture of a teaspoon of cayenne pepper and a teaspoon of superfine (caster) sugar.

Shake the pomegranate liqueur, sake, and grenadine with ice. Strain into the glass. Top up with champagne. Stir.

Wasabi Bliss

1¹/₃oz/4cl	vodka
²/₃oz/2cl	sake
¹/₂oz/1.5cl	fresh lime juice
¹/₂oz/1.5cl	gomme syrup
pea-sized	wasabi paste

GARNISH strip of toasted seaweed

Shake all ingredients and strain into a chilled cocktail glass. Float the garnish on the drink.

wine champagne fruits spices herbs
bitters vegetables fruits
wine wine sweet & creamy wine
herbs herbs champagne bitters

a to z

spices vegetables
bitters spices fruits unusual wine
herbs spices bitters
vegetables champagne
wine herbs

of flavors

bitters

In the classic cocktail sense, the word "bitters" is associated with bitter flavors created by combining herbs, roots, and other botanicals. Dating back to pre-Medieval times when herbalists mixed up medications that needed disguising before drinking, bitter flavors still retain that herbal connotation. Nosing some of the mixtures in the bottle makes you wrinkle your nose up at the bitter aromas. However, once you have braved a sip, you might surprise yourself and develop a taste for them.

The body needs the taste of bitter to stimulate the various metabolic processes associated with cleansing the liver and the digestive system, which in turn helps the body better assimilate vitamins and minerals. **Bitter flavors also stimulate the appetite** by triggering receptor sites on the tongue, which are taste buds especially designed to receive the bitter flavors.

A bitter cocktail is, by its name, not sweet, but bitter to the tongue. Some bitter flavors can be a shock to the palate, but the good thing is that they contain less sugar and less fruit pulp than other spirits or liqueurs.

Hangover cures use bitters, and when your stomach isn't in the best condition, bitters such as Fernet Branca, Underberg, or Jägermeister are a useful drink. These family-originated herbal recipes are kept a secret. For instance, Jägermeister is made from a mixture of 56 roots, barks, blossoms, and herbs, including cinammon bark, cloves, bitter oranges from Australia, ginger roots from South Asia, saffron from Spain, and coriander fruits. The combination is then macerated, blended, stored in wooden vats, then filtered before bottling. The same production methods apply to other brands of bitters. The final flavors differ, but all are bitter.

Bitter cocktail ingredients include almond liqueur, tonic water, Campari, Punt e Mes, Aperol, Cynar, Anis, Pernod, Peychaud (an orange-flavored bitters produced in New Orleans), and Angostura bitters, as well as those previously mentioned digestives.

Traditionally used in many of the early classic cocktail recipes, these older brands are undergoing a modern makeover as their owners attempt to capture the unsuspecting palates of the youth market, who have grown up on sweet colas. This is a challenge but surely a worthwhile one.

In the recipes that follow you will discover some classics and some newer combinations destined to improve your digestion and educate your palate.

aperol

Bella Taormina

1oz/3cl	gin
²/₃oz/2cl	Aperol
¹/₂oz/1.5cl	limoncello
¹/₂oz/1.5cl	mandarine liqueur
²/₃oz/2cl	fresh orange juice

GARNISH lime spiral

Shake all ingredients with ice. Strain into a chilled cocktail glass. Add the garnish.

Friends

1oz/3cl	Aperol
1oz/3cl	gin
1oz/3cl	dry vermouth

GARNISH twist of lemon

Pour ingredients into a mixing glass filled with ice. Stir. Strain into a chilled cocktail glass. Squeeze the twist of lemon into the drink, then drop it in the drink.

Gillia

2oz/6cl	Aperol
1oz/3cl	Scotch whisky

GARNISH twist of orange

Pour ingredients into a mixing glass with ice. Stir. Strain into a chilled cocktail glass. Add the garnish.

campari

Amico

1¹/₃oz/4cl	tequila
1oz/3cl	Campari
1oz/3cl	pink grapefruit juice
¹/₂oz/1.5cl	fresh lime juice
¹/₂oz/1.5cl	agave syrup

GARNISH wedge of grapefruit

Shake all ingredients with ice. Strain into an old-fashioned glass filled with ice.

Bittersweet Experiment

1oz/3cl	Campari
1oz/3cl	gin
1/2oz/1.5cl	fresh lime juice
1/2oz/1.5cl	elderflower cordial
1 tsp	clear honey
dash	egg white
	club soda

GARNISH wedge of lime

Shake all ingredients, except the soda. Strain into a highball filled with ice. Top up with soda. Stir. Add the garnish. Serve with a straw.

Bloodhound

1oz/3cl	Campari
1/2oz/1.5cl	vodka
4oz/12cl	fresh grapefruit juice

GARNISH wedge of lime

Shake all ingredients with ice. Strain into a highball filled with ice. Add the garnish.

Brother

1^1/2/4cl	tequila
1oz/3cl	Campari
1oz/3cl	pink grapefruit juice
1/2oz/1.5cl	fresh lime juice
1/2oz/1.5cl	agave syrup

GARNISH wedge of grapefruit

Shake all ingredients with ice. Strain into an old-fashioned glass with ice. Add the garnish.

Campari Nobile

1oz/3cl	vodka
2/3oz/2cl	Campari
1/3oz/1cl	limoncello
2^1/3oz/7cl	orange juice
1oz/3cl	raspberry purée
	bitter lemon

GARNISH 2 raspberries, mint leaf, slice of orange

Pour all ingredients, except bitter lemon, into a shaker with ice. Shake. Strain into a highball filled with ice. Top up with bitter lemon. Stir. Add the garnish on top of the drink. Serve with a straw and a stirrer.

Diamond Dog

1oz/3cl	Campari
1oz/3cl	dry vermouth
1oz/3cl	Rose's lime cordial
1oz/3cl	fresh orange juice

GARNISH slice of orange

Shake all ingredients with ice. Strain into an old-fashioned glass with ice.

Diana's Bitter

2oz/6cl	Plymouth gin
1oz/3cl	Campari
1oz/3cl	fresh lime juice
$1/2$oz/1.5cl	gomme syrup

GARNISH wedge of lime

Shake all ingredients with ice. Strain into a chilled cocktail glass. Add the garnish.

Garibaldi

$1^3/4$oz/5cl	Campari
$3^1/3$oz/10cl	fresh orange juice

GARNISH half slice of orange

Pour the Campari, then the orange juice, directly into an old-fashioned glass filled with ice. Stir. Add a slice of orange.

Maiori Magic

$1^1/3$oz/4cl	Campari
$2/3$oz/2cl	limoncello
$2/3$oz/2cl	fresh lemon juice
	tonic water

GARNISH wedge of lime

Pour the Campari into a highball filled with ice. Add the limoncello and lemon juice. Top up with tonic water. Stir. Squeeze a wedge of lime over the drink, then drop it in.

Marked Man

1oz/3cl	Maker's Mark bourbon
1/3oz/1cl	Campari
1/3oz/1cl	limoncello
1/2oz/1.5cl	orange juice
3	fresh mint leaves
	slice of fresh ginger

GARNISH few sticks of ginger

 Muddle the mint and ginger in the bottom of a shaker. Add ice and remaining ingredients. Shake well. Strain into a chilled cocktail glass. Balance the few sticks of ginger on the rim of the glass.

Monza

1oz/3cl	vodka
1oz/3cl	Campari
3oz/9cl	apple juice
dash	gomme syrup
1	passion fruit

GARNISH slice of apple

 Shake all ingredients with ice. Strain into a highball filled with ice. Add the garnish.

Negroni

1oz/3cl	Campari
1oz/3cl	gin
1oz/3cl	sweet vermouth
	club soda (optional)

GARNISH quarter slice of orange

 Pour all ingredients into an old-fashioned glass filled with ice. Stir. Add soda if required. Add the garnish in the drink.

Spirit Lifter

1oz/3cl	Cointreau
1oz/3cl	Campari
1oz/3cl	fresh orange juice

 Shake all ingredients with ice. Strain into a chilled cocktail glass.

fernet branca

Apothecary Cocktail

1oz/3cl	Fernet Branca
1oz/3cl	white crème de menthe
1oz/3cl	Punt e Mes

Pour all ingredients into a mixing glass with ice. Stir. Strain into a chilled cocktail glass.

Body & Soul Reviver

1oz/3cl	Branca Menthe
1oz/3cl	cognac
dash	orange bitters

Shake all ingredients with ice. Strain into a shot glass.

Corpse Reviver 3

1oz/3cl	brandy
1oz/3cl	white crème de menthe
1oz/3cl	Fernet Branca

Pour all ingredients into a mixing glass with ice. Stir. Strain into a chilled cocktail glass.

Fernet Cocktail

2/3oz/2cl	brandy
2/3oz/2cl	Fernet Branca
1 dash	Angostura bitters
2 dashes	gomme syrup

Pour ingredients into a mixing glass filled with ice. Stir. Strain into a chilled cocktail glass. Add the garnish in the drink.

GARNISH twist of lemon

A **Marked Man** has sticks of ginger as a garnish, giving a hint of spice on the nose.

fruits

This section is a celebration of fresh, seasonal, handpicked fruit produce that can be used to make a cocktail. Fruit comes in many flavors ranging from sweet and sharp to delicate and slightly bitter. From the humble green apple and citrus fruits to summer stone fruits such as apricots and deep red cherries, the selection of fruits in these recipes is deliciously tempting.

Seasonal delights abound in nature's food year, so always look for the freshest at your local farmer's market or quality supermarket.

In cocktails, freshness means the finest flavor. If the fruit is in a punnet or covered in plastic, look through the container to ensure there are no moldy pieces of fruit hidden away on the bottom. Wash and pat dry fruit such as blueberries, blackberries, apples, and pears. Raspberries don't respond well to being washed in water so try to find fresh berries that have not been sprayed.

Fresh strawberries should be washed lightly before use, then you can use a strawberry huller to get rid of the leaves.

When using fruit in a cocktail, the recipe will require you either to muddle the fruit in the bottom of a shaker or a heavy-bottomed glass, or to blend the ingredients until smooth. Fruit is muddled to release the flavor. The juice and pieces of a muddled fruit add texture to a cocktail and a visual surprise in a glass.

For purity, you might also like to place blended fruit in a muslin cloth to strain out any extraneous fiber or seeds.

When the fresh fruit is not in season, fruit from a can, or a fruit juice, can replace the real thing, but these ingredients will create a cocktail with a different flavor. If you can, use frozen fruit purée.

Before you order a drink, consider whether or not the fruit in the cocktail recipe is in season. If it's not, try a flavor that is, and you might be amused at its newness.

In the pages that follow you will find some superb fruit-flavored cocktails with more than a little hint of pleasure for the palate.

acai berry

The flavor is hard to pinpoint. Some brands of juice have been compared to bitter raspberries with a hint of cocoa bean. The Amazon's Acai is the newest berry to hit the market and is packed with much more antioxidant power than red grapes.

Acai Martini

1²/₃oz/5cl	vodka
²/₃oz/2cl	triple sec
1oz/3cl	acai berry juice

Shake all ingredients with ice. Strain into a chilled cocktail glass.

Acai Punch

SERVES 4

8oz/24cl	red wine
2 pts/75cl	acai berry juice
1 each	lime, lemon, orange, sliced
6 sprigs	fresh mint
3oz/9cl	orange juice
	soda water

GARNISH sprig of mint

Combine all ingredients, except orange juice, in a large pitcher with 2 sprigs of mint. Stir. Refrigerate for an hour. Just before you are ready to serve, add the orange juice and a large scoop of crushed ice. Stir. Serve in a highball. Top up with a little soda water. Add a sprig of mint to each glass.

Zenith

1oz/3cl	lemon vodka
¹/₂oz/1.5cl	green tea liqueur
¹/₃oz/1cl	fresh lemon juice
¹/₃oz/1cl	lemongrass stick
1oz/3cl	organic acai berry juice

GARNISH lemongrass, twist of lemon

Shake all ingredients with ice. Strain into chilled cocktail glass. Garnish with the lemongrass stick and a twist of lemon.

apple

The Granny Smith, Golden Delicious, and Braeburn are good to use in cocktails because of the balance of sweet and sour flavors. Look for firm, juicy flesh, and crispness. Apples go well with brandy, calvados, cinnamon, blackberries, and vanilla.

Apple-tini

2oz/6cl	vodka
²/₃oz/2cl	apple sour liqueur
¹/₃oz/1cl	Cointreau

GARNISH apple fan

Shake all ingredients with ice.
Strain into a chilled cocktail glass.
Add the garnish on the rim.

Appleton Garden

2oz/6cl	rum
1oz/3cl	fresh lime juice
1oz/3cl	sweet vermouth
4oz/12cl	apple juice

GARNISH ground cinnamon

Shake all ingredients with ice.
Strain into a highball filled with ice.
Sprinkle freshly ground cinnamon
over the top of the drink.

Va-Va-Voom

1²/₃oz/5cl	vodka
¹/₂oz/1.5cl	passion fruit syrup
3oz/9cl	apple juice
¹/₂oz/1.5cl	lime juice
4	fresh mint leaves

GARNISH apple fan, sprig of mint

Shake all ingredients with ice.
Strain into a highball filled with
crushed ice. Add the garnish.

apricot

The flavor of this small and perfectly formed fruit is sweet and juicy, with lush flesh designed to melt in the mouth. The fragrance is elegant. Use apricot liqueur or juice with saffron, vanilla, hazelnut liqueur, and chocolate.

Angel Face

1oz/3cl	gin
1oz/3cl	apricot brandy
1oz/3cl	calvados

 Shake all ingredients with ice.
Strain into a chilled cocktail glass.

Apricot Cosmo

1²/₃oz/5cl	vodka
¹/₂oz/1.5cl	cranberry juice
¹/₂oz/1.5cl	fresh lime juice
¹/₂oz/1.5cl	apricot brandy
1 tsp	apricot jam

GARNISH twist of orange

 Shake all ingredients with ice.
Strain into a chilled cocktail glass.
Add the garnish.

Apricot Sour

1oz/3cl	vodka
1oz/3cl	apricot brandy
2 tsps	apricot jam
1oz/3cl	fresh lemon juice
dash	egg white

GARNISH slivers of dried apricot

 Shake all ingredients with ice.
Strain into a chilled cocktail glass.
Drop slivers of dried apricot over
the top of drink.

Golden Dawn

²/₃oz/2cl	gin
²/₃oz/2cl	apricot brandy
²/₃oz/2cl	calvados
²/₃oz/2cl	fresh orange juice
dash	grenadine

Shake all ingredients, except grenadine, with ice. Strain into a chilled cocktail glass. Add the grenadine to create a sunrise effect.

Naked Lady

1oz/3cl	light rum
1oz/3cl	apricot brandy
¹/₂oz/1.5cl	fresh lemon juice
dash	grenadine

GARNISH maraschino cherry

Shake all ingredients with ice. Strain into a chilled cocktail glass. Add the garnish.

Southern Sea Breeze

1oz/3cl	bourbon
²/₃oz/2cl	apricot brandy
¹/₂oz/1.5cl	fresh lemon juice
dash	gomme syrup
2	dried apricots
1	dried fig

GARNISH dried apricot, fig

Muddle the apricots and the fig in the bottom of a shaker with the gomme. Add the remaining ingredients and ice. Shake well. double strain into an old-fashioned glass filled with ice. Add small pieces of dried apricot and fig on a toothpick across the glass.

banana

Pale-fleshed and sweet bananas bring a delicate texture and flavor to a cocktail. Bananas are great for blending in combination with spirits, juices, and liqueurs.

B B

1oz/3cl	vodka
1oz/3cl	crème de banane
1/2oz/1.5cl	white crème de cacao
1 tsp	clear honey
1oz/3cl	heavy (double) cream

GARNISH single honeysuckle blossom

 Shake all ingredients with ice. Strain into a chilled cocktail glass. Add the honeysuckle.

Banana Batida

2oz/6cl	cachaça
1oz/3cl	crème de banane
1/2oz/1.5cl	fresh lime juice
1	banana, peeled

GARNISH slice of banana, maraschino cherry

 Blend all ingredients until smooth. Add a scoop of crushed ice. Blend for ten seconds more. Pour into a highball. Add the garnish on top of the drink. Serve with a straw.

Banana Blaze

1²/3oz/5cl	cognac
1oz/3cl	crème de banane
dash	orange bitters
1	cinnamon stick
few	cloves
few	star anise

GARNISH twist of orange

 Place the spices in a small muslin bag and tie securely. Pour the ingredients into a small saucepan. Add the spices. Warm through. Take from the heat. Pour into a heat-proof glass and light the top of the drink. Let it blaze for a few seconds, then snuff it out. Add the garnish.

Banana Daiquiri

1¹/₃oz/4cl	light rum
²/₃oz/2cl	banana liqueur
¹/₃oz/1cl	fresh lime juice
1	small banana, skinned and diced

Blend all ingredients for 10 seconds. Add a small scoop crushed ice. Blend again. Pour into a chilled double cocktail glass. Add the garnish on the rim.

GARNISH small slice of banana

Beach Babe

1²/₃oz/5cl	golden rum
¹/₂oz/1.5cl	banana liqueur
2oz/6cl	fresh orange juice
1	banana, peeled and diced
2	dashes orange bitters

Blend all ingredients until smooth. Add a scoop of crushed ice. Blend again for 10 seconds. Pour into a highball. Top up with crushed ice. Stir. Add the garnish.

GARNISH physalis

Slipslider

1oz/3cl	crème de banane
¹/₂oz/2cl	Frangelico
¹/₂oz/1.5cl	Irish cream liqueur

Pour each ingredient in the order listed into a shot glass.

White Sandy Beach *nonalcoholic

3oz/9cl	pineapple juice
1²/₃oz/5cl	coconut cream
1	small ripe banana
¹/₂oz/1.5cl	heavy (double) cream

Blend all ingredients with a scoop of crushed ice until smooth. Pour the mixture into a chilled tumbler. Add the banana pieces on a cocktail stick across the glass. Add a fine sprinkle of nutmeg over the drink.

GARNISH 3 pieces of banana, ground nutmeg

blackberry

Best picked when they are plump and soft, blackberries are delicious fresh. Blackberry liqueur (crème de mûre) is also a desirable ingredient in a cocktail—try the Kir and Kir Royale.

Blackberry Margarita

1²/₃oz/5cl	aged (añejo) tequila
1oz/3cl	blackberry liqueur
1oz/3cl	fresh lime juice

GARNISH 2 blackberries, mint leaf

 Shake all ingredients with ice. Strain into an old-fashioned glass filled with crushed ice. Add the garnish on a cocktail stick. Serve with a straw.

Bonnie Fizz

1oz/3cl	gin
5	blackberries
¹/₃oz/1cl	fresh lemon juice
¹/₃oz/1cl	gomme syrup
¹/₃oz/1cl	crème de mûre
	champagne

GARNISH 3 blackberries, sprig of mint

 Muddle the berries with the syrup in a shaker. Add the remaining ingredients, except champagne. Add ice, and shake well. Strain into a highball filled with ice. Top up with champagne. Then add the crème de mûre on top. Add the garnish on a cocktail stick.

Effen Delicious

1¹/₃oz/4cl	vodka
¹/₂oz/1.5cl	crème de mûre
¹/₃oz/1cl	Bénédictine
1	fresh passion fruit
5	blackberries

GARNISH 2 blackberries, mint leaf

 Muddle the blackberries in the bottom of a shaker. Add the remaining ingredients and ice. Shake. Strain into a chilled cocktail glass. Add the garnish.

Godfrey

1oz/3cl	cognac
1/2oz/1.5cl	Grand Marnier
1/2oz/1.5cl	crème de mûre
1/3oz/1 cl	fresh lemon juice
4	blackberries

GARNISH 2 blackberries, mint leaf

 Shake all ingredients with ice. Strain into an old-fashioned glass filled with ice. Add the garnish on a cocktail stick.

Sexy Spring Punch

1/2oz/1.5cl	vodka
4	blackberries
1/2oz/1.5cl	crème de mûre
1/2oz/1.5cl	fresh lemon juice
	champagne

GARNISH slice of lemon, blackberry

 Muddle the berries in the bottom of a shaker. Add ice and remaining ingredients except champagne. Shake. Strain into a highball filled with ice. Top up with champagne. Stir. Add the garnish.

Tantric Jam

quarter	kiwi fruit
3 dashes	orange bitters
5	fresh blackberries
2oz/6cl	gin
dash	peach liqueur

GARNISH blackberry

 Muddle the fruit in the bottom of a shaker. Add ice. Add remaining ingredients. Shake well to combine the flavors. Strain into an old-fashioned glass filled with crushed ice. Top up with peach liqueur. Add the garnish. Serve with a straw.

black currant

With a shiny purple-black coating, these berries are deceptively sour and require sugar to temper their taste. However, crème de cassis, the black currant liqueur, is just sweet enough.

Back in Black

2oz/6cl	black currant-infused aged rum
⅓oz/1cl	port
⅓oz/1cl	crème de cassis
3oz/9cl	black currant tea
	club soda

GARNISH fresh black berries, sprig of black currant leaves

To infuse the rum: Add 50 black currant berries in half a bottle of aged rum. Leave a few days for the flavors to combine.

Make the tea and let cool for ten minutes. Shake all ingredients, except soda, with ice. Strain into a highball filled with ice. Top up with soda water. Add the garnish.

Black Door

1oz/3cl	black currant vodka
3	fresh black currants
⅔oz/2cl	fresh lime juice
½oz/1.5cl	crème de cassis

GARNISH orange twist, sprig of black currants

Muddle the black currants in a shaker. Add ice. Add remaining ingredients. Shake well. Strain into a chilled cocktail glass. Add the garnish on the side of the glass.

Brazilian Berry

1oz/3cl	cachaça
4	black currants
3	raspberries
2oz/6cl	white wine, dry
¹/₂oz/1.5cl	crème de cassis

Muddle the fruit in the bottom of the shaker. Add ice and the remaining ingredients. Shake. Strain into an old-fashioned glass filled with crushed ice. Serve with a straw.

High Heel

1oz/3cl	vodka
6	black currants
3	raspberries
¹/₂oz/1.5cl	crème de cassis
dash	fresh lemon juice

Shake all ingredients sharply with ice to break down the fruit. Strain into an old-fashioned glass filled with crushed ice. Add the three black currants on top of the drink.

GARNISH three black currants

Russian Spring Punch

1oz/3cl	vodka
²/₃oz/2cl	crème de cassis
¹/₂oz/1.5cl	fresh lemon juice
2 dashes	gomme syrup
	champagne

Shake all ingredients, except champagne, into a highball filled with crushed ice. Top up with champagne. Stir. Serve with a straw.

blueberry

A native North American berry, the blueberry has plump, sweet flesh and gives great juice when muddled. Full of antioxidants and vitamin C the blueberry is also thought to have anti-aging effects.

Blueberry Caipirinha

2oz/6cl	cachaça
15	blueberries
half	lime, diced
1½ tsp	superfine (caster) sugar

GARNISH 5 blueberries

Juice the blueberries. Pour the liquid into a glass and set aside. Muddle the lime in the bottom of an old-fashioned glass. Add the blueberry juice, sugar, and the cachaça. Add crushed ice. Add five blueberries to the drink. Stir. Serve with a straw.

Blueberry Muffin Martini

1oz/3cl	vodka
½oz/1.5cl	vanilla vodka
½oz/1.5cl	blueberry liqueur
½oz/1.5cl	white crème de cacao
3	fresh blueberries

GARNISH 4 blueberries, vanilla stick

Shake all ingredients sharply with ice. Double strain into a cocktail glass. Thread the blueberries with the vanilla stick and place on the edge of the glass..

Blueberry Rocket

1oz/3cl	light rum
10	blueberries
½oz/1.5cl	blueberry liqueur
1oz/3cl	fresh lime juice
dash	vanilla sugar syrup

GARNISH 3 blueberries

Muddle the blueberries in the bottom of a shaker. Add remaining ingredients and ice. Shake sharply. Double strain into a chilled cocktail glass. Drop the three blueberries in the drink.

Blueberry Muffin Martini is enhanced by the novel garnish set across the glass.

cherry

Both sweet and sour varieties are rich in antioxidants. The maraschino and Morello sour cherries are used to make kirsch liqueur, and the maraschino is familiar as the red cocktail cherry.

Blood & Sand

1oz/3cl	Scotch whisky
2/3oz/2cl	cherry brandy
2/3oz/2cl	sweet vermouth
1oz/3cl	fresh blood orange juice

GARNISH twist of orange

Shake all ingredients with ice. Strain into a chilled cocktail glass. Squeeze and then drop the garnish in the drink.

Bookmark

1 2/3oz/5cl	bourbon
8	pitted Morello cherries
1/3oz/1cl	cinnamon syrup
1/2oz/1.5cl	vintage port
2 dashes	Angostura bitters

GARNISH twist of orange

Add the bourbon, syrup, port, and bitters to a mixing glass and stir while gradually adding ice cubes. Muddle the cherries in an old-fashioned glass. Add ice cubes. Strain the contents of the mixing glass into the old-fashioned glass. Stir. Add the garnish.

Cherry Blossom

1oz/3cl	cognac
2/3oz/2cl	cherry brandy
1/2oz/1.5cl	maraschino liqueur
1/2oz/1.5cl	orange curaçao
1/2oz/1.5cl	fresh lemon juice

GARNISH red maraschino cherry

Shake all ingredients with ice. Strain into a chilled cocktail glass. Drop the garnish in the drink.

Cherry Crush

2oz/6cl	gin
1oz/3cl	maraschino liqueur
4	sweet cherries, pitted
$^{1}/_{2}$oz/1.5cl	fresh lemon juice

GARNISH fresh red cherry

Muddle the cherries in the bottom of a shaker. Add remaining ingredients and ice. Shake. Double strain into a chilled cocktail glass. Drop the cherry into the drink.

Pop-a-Cherry-tini

1$^{2}/_{3}$oz/5cl	passion fruit vodka
$^{1}/_{2}$oz/1.5cl	cherry brandy
$^{1}/_{2}$oz/1.5cl	crème de framboise
$^{2}/_{3}$oz/2cl	fresh lime juice
half	fresh passion fruit
2 tsps	demerara sugar
2	small bunches fresh oregano
6	ripe cherries

GARNISH fresh red cherry, sprig of oregano

Pit the cherries and place them in a shaker with the sugar and the oregano. Muddle. Add ice and the remaining ingredients. Shake. Double strain into a chilled cocktail glass. Add the garnish on the side of the glass.

Singapore Sling

1$^{2}/_{3}$oz/5cl	gin
$^{1}/_{2}$oz/1.5cl	cherry brandy
$^{1}/_{3}$oz/1cl	Bénédictine
$^{1}/_{3}$oz/1cl	Cointreau
$^{1}/_{3}$oz/1cl	fresh lemon juice
$^{2}/_{3}$oz/2cl	orange juice
1oz/3cl	pineapple juice

GARNISH wedge of lime, fresh red cherry

Shake all ingredients with ice. Pour into a highball filled with crushed ice. Add the garnish to a cocktail stick and place it in the drink.

coconut

Coconut milk is soft in the mouth and has a fruity, nutty flavor.
For cocktails you can use coconut cream or coconut milk, or a
coconut-flavored spirit such as rum.

Big Jim Knockout Punch

1oz/3cl	dark rum
¹/₂oz/1.5cl	pineapple rum
¹/₂oz/1.5cl	coconut rum
4oz/12cl	fresh orange juice
dash	grenadine
¹/₂oz/1.5cl	coconut cream

GARNISH slice of orange, sprig of mint

Shake all ingredients with ice.
Strain into a highball filled with ice.
Add the garnish on top of the drink.

Coco Affair *nonalcoholic

1oz/3cl	coconut cream
1¹/₃oz/4cl	fresh orange juice
1¹/₃oz/4cl	pineapple juice
6	fresh strawberries, diced
¹/₂oz/1.5cl	heavy (double) cream

GARNISH half a strawberry

Blend all ingredients until smooth,
add a scoop of crushed ice and
blend again. Pour into a highball or
a tumbler. Add the garnish on the
rim. Serve with a straw.

Cococabana

1oz/3cl	coconut rum
1oz/3cl	melon liqueur
3¹/₃oz/10cl	pineapple juice
1oz/3cl	coconut cream

GARNISH slice of star fruit

Blend all ingredients with a scoop
of crushed ice until smooth. Pour
into a goblet. Add the garnish on
the rim. Serve with a straw.

Piña Colada

1²/₃oz/5cl	light rum
3¹/₃oz/10cl	pineapple juice
1²/₃oz/5cl	coconut cream
	crushed ice

GARNISH slice of pineapple, maraschino cherry

Pour the pineapple juice into a blender. Add the coconut cream and the rum. Blend for a few seconds. Add the crushed ice and blend for five seconds. Pour into a colada glass or a goblet. Add the garnish on a cocktail stick on the rim.

Pirate's Sip

1oz/3cl	coconut rum
1oz/3cl	dark overproof rum
2oz/6cl	coconut cream
1oz/3cl	fresh lime juice

GARNISH wedge of pineapple, red cherry

Blend all ingredients with crushed ice. Pour into a colada glass. Add the garnish on the rim.

Possibility

1²/₃oz/5cl	vanilla vodka
¹/₂oz/1.5cl	strawberry purée
1¹/₂oz/1.5cl	coconut cream

Shake all ingredients with ice. Strain into a chilled cocktail glass.

Sensual Bay Breeze

1¹/₂oz/4.5cl	coconut rum
2oz/6cl	cranberry juice
2oz/6cl	pineapple juice

Shake all ingredients with ice. Strain into a highball filled with ice.

coffee

Freshly ground coffee flavors can differ greatly. On the tongue, sweet, salty, bitter, and sour tastes are perceived. Coffee liqueurs such as Kahlua have a thick consistency and mix well.

Black Russian

1^1/3oz/4cl	vodka
^{2}/3oz/2cl	Kahlua

Pour the vodka into an old-fashioned glass filled with ice. Add the Kahlua. Stir. Serve with a stirrer.

Espresso Martini

2oz/6cl	vodka
1oz/3cl	espresso coffee
^{1}/2oz/1.5cl	Kahlua

GARNISH 4 coffee beans

Shake all ingredients with ice. Strain into a chilled cocktail glass. Place the beans on top of the drink.

Irish Coffee

1^2/3oz/5cl	Irish whiskey
2 tsps	brown sugar
3oz/9cl	hot coffee
^{2}/3oz/2cl	whipped cream

Pour the whiskey into a heat-proof glass. Add the sugar and stir. Add the hot coffee and stir. Gently float the whipped cream over the back of a barspoon so it creates a creamy level on top of the drink.

Last Sin

1^2/3oz/5cl	7-year-old rum
1oz/3cl	Frangelico
^{1}/3oz/1cl	gomme syrup
1 shot	espresso coffee

GARNISH 3 coffee beans

Shake all ingredients with ice. Strain into a chilled cocktail glass. Float the beans on the surface.

Black Russian (foreground) and **Last Sin** cocktails are full of coffee flavor.

cranberry

A tart flavor is at the base of this berry's juice. Available as white and red juices, the cranberry is good to use when you want to cut the sweetness in a cocktail. It is also full of antioxidants and vitamins so you can sip a healthy drink.

Cape Cod

2oz/6cl	**vodka**
4oz/12cl	**cranberry juice**

GARNISH wedge of lime

Build the ingredients in a highball filled with ice. Stir. Add the garnish.

Devil's Butterfly

1oz/3cl	**silver tequila**
1oz/3cl	**Cointreau**
1/2oz/1.5cl	**rose syrup**
2oz/6cl	**cranberry juice**

GARNISH rose petal

Shake all ingredients with ice. Strain into a chilled cocktail glass. Add the garnish to the drink.

White Cosmopolitan

1²/3oz/5cl	**vodka**
1/3oz/1cl	**Cointreau**
1/3oz/1cl	**white cranberry juice**
1/3oz/1cl	**fresh lime juice**

GARNISH lime twist

Shake all ingredients with ice. Strain into a chilled cocktail glass. Add the garnish.

fig

Another seasonal luxury fruit, fresh figs have a delicate musky flavor when ripe. Best eaten at room temperature, figs add sensuality to a cocktail's flavor. Look for fruit that yields, but is not squashy, to the touch.

Fickle Fig

1²/₃oz/5cl	grappa	
2	fresh figs, diced and skinned	
dash	grenadine	
teaspoon	honey	
	prosecco (Italian sparkling wine)	

Lightly muddle the figs in the bottom of a shaker. Add ice, and remaining ingredients, except the prosecco. Shake. Strain into a chilled champagne coupe glass. Top up with prosecco. Stir.

Fig Supreme

2oz/6cl	añejo (aged) tequila
¹/₂oz/1.5cl	fresh lime juice
¹/₂oz/1.5cl	Grand Marnier
dash	grenadine
1	ripe, dark fig, peeled and diced

Gently muddle the fig with the lime juice and grenadine in the bottom of a shaker. Add ice. Shake well. Strain into an old-fashioned glass filled with crushed ice. Add the garnish on the rim.

GARNISH neat wedge of fig

Sweet Indulgence

2oz/6cl	reposado tequila
1	fresh fig, flesh removed
1 tsp	honey
¹/₂oz/2cl	hot water
1oz/3cl	fresh lime juice

Muddle the fig with the hot water and honey. Add the remaining ingredients. Add ice. Shake. Strain into a chilled cocktail glass. Add the garnish.

GARNISH wedge of fig

grapefruit

There are three types of grapefruit flesh: white, pink, and ruby.
Each flavor is different but they all are slightly sharp, with a hint
of sweetness. The fruit is excellent for fresh juice and as a garnish.

Bacardi Grapefruit Blossom

1¹/₃oz/4cl	Bacardi rum
1¹/₃oz/4cl	grapefruit juice
2 dashes	maraschino liqueur

Shake all ingredients with ice.
Strain into a chilled cocktail glass.

Bitter Kiss

1oz/3cl	vodka
1oz/3cl	ruby red grapefruit juice
2 dashes	Angostura bitters
	champagne

Shake all ingredients, except
champagne, with ice. Pour into a
champagne flute. Stir.

Morning Margarita

1²/₃oz/5cl	tequila
¹/₂oz/1.5cl	Cointreau
1oz/3cl	pink grapefruit juice
¹/₂oz/1.5cl	fresh lemon juice
1 tsp	medium-cut orange
	marmalade
1 tsp	agave syrup

GARNISH strips of grapefruit peel

Shake all ingredients with ice
sharply so that the flavor of the
marmalade is released. Strain into
an old-fashioned glass filled with
ice. Add the grapefruit peel garnish
on top of the drink.

Papa Doble

1²/₃oz/5cl	rum	
¹/₃oz/1cl	maraschino liqueur	
²/₃oz/2cl	fresh grapefruit juice	
¹/₃oz/1cl	gomme syrup	
¹/₂oz/1.5cl	fresh lime juice	

 Blend all ingredients with a little ice. Pour into a wine glass. Add the garnish on a cocktail stick.

GARNISH wedge of lime, maraschino cherry

Sal's Tart

2oz/6cl	vanilla vodka
¹/₂oz/1.5cl	fresh lime juice
1 tsp	clear honey
1oz/3cl	pink grapefruit juice

 Shake all ingredients with ice. Strain into a chilled cocktail glass. Add the garnish.

GARNISH grapefruit spiral

Salty Dog

2oz/6cl	vodka
¹/₂oz/1.5cl	fresh lime juice

 Salt the rim of a highball. Fill it with ice. Add the ingredients. Stir.

You're So Cool *nonalcoholic

2oz/6cl	pink grapefruit juice
¹/₂oz/1.5cl	raspberry purée
half	fresh passion fruit
dash	grenadine
	club soda

Shake all ingredients, except soda, with ice. Strain into a highball filled with ice. Add the garnish on a cocktail stick.

GARNISH quarter slice of passion fruit, sprig of mint

kiwi fruit

Under its brown, fuzzy protective coating lies a soft, delectable, bright green flesh that's ready to eat. Its taste is a combination of sweet and tart when ripe. Look for fruit that's soft to the touch.

Kiwi Daiquiri

1¹/₃oz/4cl	light rum
1oz/3cl	fresh lime juice
1	kiwi fruit, peeled and diced

GARNISH slice of kiwi fruit

Crust a cocktail glass rim with sugar. Blend all ingredients with a handful of ice for 30 seconds until smooth. Strain into the glass. Add the kiwi fruit on the rim.

Kiwi Delight *nonalcoholic

SERVES 6	
6	kiwi fruit, peeled and diced
2oz/6cl	gomme syrup
3oz/9cl	fresh lemon juice
	mineral water

GARNISH wedge of kiwi fruit

Blend the kiwi fruit, gomme, and lemon juice until smooth. Add a scoop of crushed ice. Blend again. Fill four highballs with crushed ice and strain the mixture into each glass. Top up with mineral water. Add the garnish.

Voodoo Breeze

1²/₃oz/5cl	gold tequila
²/₃oz/2cl	melon liqueur
3oz/9cl	fresh apple juice
¹/₃oz/1cl	fresh lime juice
1	fresh kiwi

GARNISH thin slice of kiwi

Scoop out the pulp of a ripe kiwi. Muddle in the bottom of a shaker. Add ice and remaining ingredients. Shake. Strain over crushed ice into a highball. Add the garnish.

The color and fragrance of **Voodoo Breeze** capture the eye and the palate.

lemon

The lemon is a versatile fruit that's an essential ingredient because of its sharp flavor. Its fresh juice balances sweet liqueurs and syrups, and adds its own piquancy. Use it as a twist, a slice, a spiral, and a wedge, plus you can grate the rind over a drink.

Bella Donna

1²/₃oz/5cl	light rum
²/₃oz/2cl	limoncello
1¹/₃oz/4cl	fresh lemon juice
dash	champagne
dash	rose syrup

GARNISH lemon spiral

 Shake all ingredients, except champagne, with ice. Strain into a chilled cocktail glass. Top up with champagne. Add the lemon spiral.

Horny Toad

1oz/3cl	silver tequila
²/₃oz/2cl	Cointreau
1¹/₃oz/4cl	fresh lemon juice

 Prepare a margarita glass with a crusted rim. Shake all ingredients with ice. Strain into the glass filled with crushed ice.

Lemon Drop

1¹/₂oz/4.5cl	vodka
²/₃oz/2cl	fresh lemon juice
barspoon	gomme syrup

GARNISH twist of lemon

 Prepare the rim of the cocktail glass with a sugar crust. Shake all ingredients with ice. Strain into a chilled cocktail glass.

Lemon Gin Collins

1oz/3cl	gin
1/3oz/1cl	gomme syrup
3/4oz/2.5cl	limoncello
1/2oz/1.5cl	fresh lemon juice
	club soda

 Shake all ingredients, except soda, with ice. Strain into a highball filled with ice. Stir. Squeeze a wedge of lemon over the drink and drop it in. Serve with two straws.

Lemon Meringue

1²/3oz/5cl	lemon vodka
1/2oz/1.5cl	Drambuie
1oz/3cl	fresh lemon juice
dash	gomme syrup

GARNISH shredded lemon peel

 Shake all ingredients with ice. Strain into a chilled cocktail glass. Add the garnish on top of the drink.

Vodka Sour

1²/3oz/5cl	vodka
2/3oz/2cl	fresh lemon juice
1	pasteurized egg white
dash	gomme syrup

GARNISH maraschino cherry, slice of orange

 Shake all ingredients with ice. Strain into a cocktail glass. Add the garnish on a cocktail stick.

Whiskey Sour

2oz/6cl	bourbon
1/2oz/1.5cl	fresh lemon juice
half tsp	gomme syrup
dash	egg white

GARNISH slice of orange

 Shake all ingredients with ice. Strain into a chilled cocktail glass. Add the garnish.

lime

The true flavor of lime is captured in this selection of classic recipes. With a more assertive, sharp flavor than lemon, the lime is the key ingredient in a Margarita, Mojito, and Daiquiri. There is nothing more purely citrus than a fresh-cut lime.

Caipirinha

1²/₃oz/5cl	cachaça
1	small fresh lime
1¹/₂ tsps	superfine (caster) sugar

Wash the lime and slice off the top and bottom. Cut into small segments from top to bottom. Add the lime slices and the sugar to an old-fashioned glass. Crush the lime to make juice, and muddle to ensure the sugar dissolves. Add ice cubes, the cachaça, and stir well. Serve with a stirrer. A straw is optional.

Daiquiri

1²/₃oz/5cl	light rum
1oz/3cl	fresh lime juice
3 dashes	gomme syrup

GARNISH wedge of lime

Shake all ingredients with ice. Strain into a chilled cocktail glass. Add the garnish.

Kamikaze Shooter

²/₃oz/2cl	chilled vodka
²/₃oz/2cl	fresh lime juice
¹/₃oz/1cl	Cointreau

Shake all ingredients with ice. Strain into a shot glass. Serve with a wedge of lime on the side. Take a bite of the lime, then drink.

Margarita

1¹/₃oz/4cl	silver tequila
³/₄oz/2.5cl	Cointreau
²/₃oz/2cl	lime juice

GARNISH slice of lime

Salt half of the rim of the glass. Shake and strain into a chilled cocktail glass. Add the garnish on the rim.

Pisco Sour

1²/₃oz/5cl	pisco (brandy from Chile/Peru)
²/₃oz/2cl	fresh lime juice
dash	egg white powder
2 dashes	Angostura bitters
dash	gomme syrup

GARNISH wedge of lime

Shake all ingredients with ice. Strain into a chilled cocktail glass. Add the garnish.

Tommy's Margarita

2oz/6cl	tequila
1oz/3cl	fresh lime juice
1 tsp	agave syrup
1 tsp	gomme syrup
1 tsp	still water

GARNISH slice of lime

Salt the rim of the glass if you desire. Stir the sugar and the water in a shaker. Add the remaining ingredients and ice. Shake. Double strain into a chilled cocktail glass. Add the garnish.

Vodka Gimlet

1²/₃oz/5cl	chilled vodka
²/₃oz/2cl	Rose's lime cordial

GARNISH thin wedge of lime

Pour the chilled vodka into an old-fashioned glass filled with ice. Add the lime cordial. Stir. Add the garnish on the rim.

lychee

Here is a subtropical fruit with white, pinkish, and translucent flesh that's glossy like a grape's. Its flavor is sweet on the tongue with a hint of fragrance. Fresh lychees can be muddled to release flavor.

Chinese Lily

1¹/₃oz/4cl	tequila
²/₃oz/2cl	lychee liqueur
²/₃oz/2cl	lychee purée
¹/₂oz/1.5cl	fresh lemon juice
dash	orgeat syrup

Shake all ingredients with ice.
Strain into a chilled cocktail glass.

Lychee Crush

1²/₃oz/5cl	golden rum
1oz/3cl	lychee liqueur
half	fresh kiwi fruit
¹/₂oz/1.5cl	fresh lemon juice
dash	gomme syrup

GARNISH fresh lychee

Shake all ingredients with ice.
Strain into a chilled cocktail glass.
Drop the lychee into the drink.

Lychee La La

2oz/6cl	gin
¹/₂oz/2cl	gomme syrup
3	lemon wedges
3	lychees
	lemongrass stem

GARNISH lemongrass stem, peeled lychee

Muddle the lychees, shredded lemongrass stem, lemon wedges with the gomme in the bottom of a shaker. Add ice and the gin. Shake well to combine the flavors. Strain into a chilled cocktail glass. Add the garnish on a cocktail stick at the side of the drink.

Lychee Lover

1²/₃oz/5cl	vodka
1oz/3cl	lychee liqueur
²/₃oz/2cl	fresh lemon juice
dash	pink grapefruit juice

GARNISH small orchid

Shake all ingredients with ice.
Strain into a chilled cocktail glass.
Add the garnish on the rim.

Lychee-tini

1²/₃oz/5cl	vodka
¹/₂oz/1.5cl	lychee liqueur
¹/₂oz/1.5cl	dry vermouth
²/₃oz/2cl	lychee juice, drained from a can of lychees

GARNISH peeled lychee

Shake all ingredients with ice.
Strain into a chilled cocktail glass.
Add the garnish on the rim.

Monte Christo

1oz/3cl	light rum
1	lime, diced
2 tsp	superfine (caster) sugar
¹/₂oz/1.5cl	lychee juice, drained from a can of lychees
¹/₂oz/1.5cl	raspberry liqueur
1oz/3cl	cranberry juice

Muddle the diced limes in the
bottom of a shaker. Add ice and
remaining ingredients. Shake well.
Add ice to a highball. Strain the
drink over ice, allowing a few lime
wedges to slip in.

North Sea Breeze

2oz/6cl	gin
2¹/₃oz/7cl	lychee juice, drained from a can of lychees
3oz/9cl	grapefruit juice

GARNISH wedge of lime

Pour the ingredients one at a time
directly into a highball filled with
ice. Squeeze the wedge of lime into
the drink and add it to the glass.

mango

Lush and full of juice, the mango has the flavor of the Caribbean in its essence. Sweet, the fresh mango is brilliant for blended cocktails. Rich in antioxidants, they are a glorious fruit.

Frescolina

2oz/6cl	vodka
2/3oz/2cl	Cointreau
1/2oz/1.5cl	mango purée
1/3oz/1cl	fresh lime juice

GARNISH wedge of mango

Shake all ingredients with ice. Double strain through a tea strainer into a chilled cocktail glass. Add the wedge on the rim.

Frozen Mango Daiquiri

1²/3oz/5cl	light rum
1/2oz/1.5cl	mango liqueur
1oz/3cl	fresh lime juice
quarter	fresh mango, peeled and diced

GARNISH small wedge of mango

Blend ingredients with a scoop of crushed ice. Pour into an old-fashioned glass. Add the garnish on the rim. Serve with a straw.

Fruity Mimosa

SERVES 6

5oz/15cl	fresh orange juice
2oz/6cl	fresh lime juice
flesh	large mango
1 bottle	prosecco (Italian sparkling wine)

Blend the mango flesh with the orange juice until smooth. Add the lime juice and a scoop of ice cubes, and blend again. Pour the mixture into a large pitcher, then slowly add the prosecco. Stir. Serve in six champagne flutes.

Mango Cosmopolitan

2oz/6cl	Malibu mango rum
¹/₂oz/1.5cl	fresh lemon juice
¹/₃oz/1cl	cranberry juice

GARNISH twist of lemon

Shake all ingredients with ice.
Strain into a chilled cocktail glass.
Add the twist.

Mango-lick

³/₄oz/2.5cl	licorice-infused cachaça
³/₄oz/2.5cl	mango-infused cachaça
1 slice	mango, diced
half	fresh lime, diced
¹/₃oz/1cl	mango liqueur

Infuse cachaça with licorice root for
one day; infuse some cachaça with
fresh, ripe mango for two days.
Muddle the mango and lime in a
mixing glass. When the juices and
the oils have combined, add
crushed ice and the cachaça and
mango liqueur. Stir well. Pour into
an old-fashioned glass.

Mangorita

1¹/₃oz/4cl	añejo (aged) tequila
²/₃oz/2cl	Grand Marnier
²/₃oz/2cl	mango purée
¹/₂oz/1.5cl	fresh lime juice
dash	agave syrup

GARNISH wedge of lime

Shake all ingredients with ice.
Strain into a chilled cocktail glass.
Add the garnish on the rim.

Tropical Drop

1oz/3cl	golden mango liqueur
¹/₂oz/1.5cl	coconut cream
¹/₂oz/1.5cl	coconut rum
4oz/12cl	pineapple juice

GARNISH slice of mango

Blend all ingredients with a scoop
of ice. Pour into a goblet filled with
ice. Add the garnish on the rim.

melon

The flavor depends on the type of melon you use. Canteloupe, honeydew, and watermelon varieties add superb sweet and juicy flavors to any cocktail, and go especially well with ginger and rum.

Cantaloupe Cup

2oz/6cl	light rum
half	fresh cantaloupe melon
$^{1}/_{2}$oz/1.5cl	fresh orange juice
$^{1}/_{2}$oz/1.5cl	fresh lime juice
dash	gomme syrup

GARNISH slice of melon

 Blend all ingredients with a small scoop of crushed ice until smooth. Pour into an old-fashioned glass filled with ice. Add the garnish.

Demon Melon

1$^{2}/_{3}$oz/5cl	sake
$^{3}/_{4}$ cup	fresh yellow-fleshed melon
2oz/6cl	gomme syrup
1oz/3cl	fresh lime juice

GARNISH melon balls of different colors

 Pour ingredients into a blender with a scoop of crushed ice. Blend until smooth. Strain into a large goblet filled with ice. Add the garnish.

Kyoto Cocktail

$^{1}/_{2}$oz/1.5cl	gin
$^{2}/_{3}$oz/2cl	melon liqueur
$^{1}/_{3}$oz/1cl	dry vermouth
1	wedge of lemon

GARNISH 3 assorted melon balls

 Add the gin, melon liqueur, and vermouth to a shaker with ice. Squeeze the juice from the lemon wedge into the shaker. Shake. Strain into a chilled cocktail glass. Add the melon balls on a cocktail stick.

Melon Babe

1²/₃oz/5cl	lemon vodka
²/₃oz/2cl	fresh lemon juice
1oz/3cl	gomme syrup
half cup	cantaloupe melon, diced
	mineral water

GARNISH twist of orange

Blend all ingredients, except mineral water, with crushed ice. Pour into a highball filled with ice. Top up with water. Add the garnish and flame it. Be careful not to burn yourself.

Melon Ball

1oz/3cl	vodka
²/₃oz/2cl	melon liqueur
3¹/₃oz/10cl	pineapple juice

GARNISH melon balls of different colors

Shake all ingredients with ice. Strain into a highball filled with ice. Garnish with a few melon balls on a cocktail stick.

Melon Patch

1²/₃oz/5cl	vodka
1oz/3cl	melon liqueur
¹/₂oz/1.5cl	triple sec
	club soda

GARNISH slice of orange

Shake the first three ingredients with ice. Strain into a highball filled with ice. Top up with club soda. Add the garnish.

Melon-tini

2oz/6cl	vodka
1¹/₂oz/4.5cl	honeydew melon juice
1¹/₂oz/4.5cl	cantaloupe melon juice

GARNISH melon ball

Make the juices by blending half of each fresh melon. Shake the melon juices and vodka with ice. Strain into a cocktail glass. Add the garnish.

olive

Black olives are more bitter than the green variety, ranging in flavor from mild to vibrant, depending on how they were cured. Green olives such as the Spanish Manzanilla are perfect for the classic gin Martini. They have a light, salty flavor.

Dirty Martini

2oz/6cl	vodka
1oz/3cl	green olive brine
dash	dry vermouth

GARNISH three green olives

Pour ingredients into a mixing glass with ice. Stir. Strain into a chilled cocktail glass. Add the garnish in the drink. If the drinker requests it not so dirty, reduce the olive brine to half, and increase the vodka by half again.

Naked New York

3oz/9cl	vodka
1/3oz/1cl	dry vermouth
few	green pitted olives

GARNISH 3 olives, slice of blue cheese

Pour the vodka into a mixing glass with ice. Add the vermouth. Stir. Pour into a cocktail glass. Stuff the olives with the blue cheese and drop them in the drink.

Personality-ini

2oz/6cl	vodka
dash	black olive juice
dash	dry vermouth

GARNISH two black olives

Add the ingredients to a mixing glass with ice. Stir until the liquid is cold and frosty. Strain into a chilled cocktail glass. Drop the two black olives in the drink.

Chilled to perfection, the cocktail glass contains the perfect **Dirty Martini** mix.

orange

Oranges can be divided into two types: bitter and sweet. The peel of bitter oranges is used to make orange curaçao liqueur. Sweet oranges are used to make fresh juice. Blood oranges are exceptionally sweet and rich in flavor.

Breakfast Martini

1²/₃oz/5cl	gin
¹/₂oz/1.5cl	Cointreau
¹/₂oz/1.5cl	fresh lemon juice
2 barspoons	thin-cut orange marmalade

GARNISH shredded orange peel

Shake the ingredients with ice. Strain into a chilled cocktail glass. Shred some orange peel on the top of the drink.

Lucy Loop

1oz/3cl	gin
²/₃oz/2cl	Aperol
¹/₂oz/1.5cl	fresh lemon juice
¹/₂oz/1.5cl	mandarin liqueur
²/₃oz/2cl	fresh orange juice

GARNISH kumquat, lime spiral

Pour all ingredients into a shaker with ice. Shake. Strain into a cocktail glass. Garnish with a kumquat cut like a flower and a spiral of lime set on the rim.

Mad Mandarin

1oz/3cl	mandarin liqueur
1oz/3cl	fresh orange juice
¹/₂oz/1.5cl	chocolate liqueur
²/₃oz/2cl	heavy (double) cream
dash	orange bitters

GARNISH orange spiral

Shake all ingredients with ice. Strain into a chilled cocktail glass.

Maiden's Prayer

1¹/₃oz/4cl	gin
²/₃oz/2cl	Cointreau
²/₃oz/2cl	fresh orange juice
¹/₃oz/1cl	fresh lemon juice

GARNISH twist of orange

 Shake all ingredients with ice. Strain into a chilled cocktail glass. Add the garnish.

Metropolis

1²/₃oz/5cl	mandarin vodka
²/₃oz/2cl	Mandarine Napoleon liqueur
²/₃oz/2cl	fresh lemon juice
¹/₂oz/1.5cl	gomme syrup

GARNISH twist of orange

 Shake all ingredients with ice. Strain into a chilled cocktail glass. Add the twist of orange.

Orange Breeze

1²/₃oz/5cl	vodka
3¹/₃oz/10cl	fresh orange juice
3¹/₃oz/10cl	apple juice
1oz/3cl	cranberry juice

GARNISH wedge of orange

 Shake all ingredients with ice. Strain into a chilled cocktail glass.

Orange-tini

2oz/6cl	gin
¹/₂oz/1.5cl	Cointreau
¹/₃oz/1cl	dry vermouth
2 dashes	orange bitters

GARNISH twist of orange

 Stir all ingredients in a mixing glass filled with ice. Strain into a chilled cocktail glass with ice. Add the twist of orange.

Pink Flamingo

2oz/6cl	mandarin vodka
1/2oz/1.5cl	Sourz apple
2/3oz/2cl	cranberry juice
1/2oz/1.5cl	fresh lime juice

GARNISH thin slice of apple

Shake all ingredients with ice. Strain into a chilled cocktail glass. Add the garnish on top of the drink.

Screwdriver

1 3/4oz/5cl	vodka
5oz/15cl	fresh orange juice

GARNISH slice of orange

Pour the vodka into a highball filled with ice. Add the orange juice. Stir well. Add the garnish in the drink. Serve with a stirrer.

Tawny Orange Jelly Sour

1 2/3oz/5cl	Hendrick's gin
1/2oz/1cl	honey syrup
2 level tsps	orange thick-cut marmalade
2/3oz/2cl	fresh lemon juice

GARNISH orange spiral, orange peel

Shake all ingredients with ice. Strain through a tea strainer into a chilled coupe glass. Drop the orange peel in the drink and place the orange spiral on the rim.

Tequila Sunrise

1 2/3oz/5cl	tequila
5oz/15cl	fresh orange juice
2 dashes	grenadine

GARNISH orange spiral

Pour the tequila and orange juice into a highball filled with ice. Stir. Splash in grenadine and watch it trickle down through the drink. Add the garnish. Serve with a straw and two stirrers.

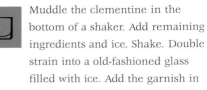

Toledo Punch

1²/₃oz/5cl	dark rum
¹/₂oz/1.5cl	dry sherry
¹/₃oz/1cl	chamomile syrup
¹/₂oz/1.5cl	mandarin liqueur
¹/₂oz/1cl	fresh lime juice
	grated nutmeg
1	clementine, diced

GARNISH 3 segments of clementine, sprig of mint

Muddle the clementine in the bottom of a shaker. Add remaining ingredients and ice. Shake. Double strain into a old-fashioned glass filled with ice. Add the garnish in the drink.

passion fruit

At first taste you think your mouth has exploded with sharp flavors, then the sweet, intense fruit comes through the juicy flesh. This is a dominant flavor in any cocktail. Strain the small black seeds if you prefer.

Bonito

1²/₃oz/5cl	tequila
¹/₂oz/1.5cl	Grand Marnier
2 barspoons	brown sugar
3	orange wedges
¹/₃oz/1cl	fresh lime juice
3oz/9cl	fresh passion fruit juice

GARNISH half a passion fruit

Muddle the orange wedges with the sugar in the bottom of a shaker. Add ice and the remaining ingredients. Shake well. Strain into a highball filled with crushed ice. Place the garnish on top of the drink. Serve with a straw.

Deep Passion

1¹/₃oz/4cl	vodka
¹/₂oz/1.5cl	Grand Marnier
3oz/9cl	passion fruit juice
1oz/3cl	fresh lime juice
1	passion fruit

GARNISH physalis

Cut the passion fruit in half, and scoop it into the shaker. Add remaining ingredients and ice. Shake. Strain into a highball filled with ice. Add the garnish on the rim of the glass.

French Passion

1²/₃oz/5cl	cognac
¹/₃oz/1cl	ginger cordial
¹/₂oz/1.5cl	passion fruit syrup
¹/₂oz/1.5cl	Mandarine Napoleon
1	fresh lime, diced
2 barspoons	superfine (caster) sugar
2	small sticks ginger
1	passion fruit
1oz/3cl	passion fruit purée

GARNISH sprig of mint set in two wheels of passion fruit, one on top of the other

Muddle the fresh lime, sugar, ginger torn into small sections, and flesh of half a passion fruit in a highball. Add the passion fruit purée, cognac, ginger cordial, and passion fruit syrup. Nearly fill the glass with crushed ice and stir well. When combined, top up with crushed ice, then pour the Mandarine Napoleon over. Add the garnish on top of the crushed ice.

Passion-tini

2oz/6cl	vodka
1oz/3cl	passion fruit purée
¹/₂oz/1.5cl	strawberry purée

Shake all ingredients with ice. Strain into a chilled cocktail glass.

Smoocher

1oz/3cl	vodka
4	passion fruit, halved
¹/₂oz/1.5cl	peach and passion fruit syrup
1 tsp	vanilla sugar

Halve the passion fruit and scoop out the pulp from all but one half. Strain out the seeds. Pour 1oz/3cl of the juice into a shaker, add the remaining ingredients and ice. Shake. Strain into a chilled cocktail glass. Garnish with the remaining half of the passion fruit.

peach

The white flesh of a fresh peach has a finer flavor than the pale yellow variety and is perfect for the classic champagne cocktail, Bellini. Sweet and fragrant, peach flavor is good when combined with raspberries, vanilla, wine, and cream.

Bellini

1oz/3cl	**white peach purée**
	prosecco (Italian
	spakling wine)

 Pour the peach into a chilled champagne flute. Top up with prosecco. Stir gently, making sure the drink is mixed.

Parisian Blossom

1¹/₃oz/4cl	**vodka**
¹/₃oz/1cl	**Peche de Vigne**
²/₃oz/2cl	**peach purée**
¹/₃oz/1cl	**fresh lemon juice**
2	**cardamom pods**

 Muddle the cardamom pods in the shaker. Add the remaining ingredients and ice. Shake. Strain into a chilled cocktail glass.

Parisian Smash

1oz/3cl	**cognac**
¹/₂oz/1.5cl	**peach liqueur**
1	**lemon wedge**
1	**orange wedge**
half	**ripe peach, crushed**
6	**mint leaves**
¹/₃oz/1cl	**sugar syrup**

 Muddle the fruit in the bottom of a shaker. Add ice and remaining ingredients. Shake. Strain into an old-fashioned glass filled with crushed ice. Add the garnish.

GARNISH wedge of peach, sprig of mint

Parisian Blossom, seen here with **Champagne & Pear Drop**, has a layer of cardamom flavor.

pear

Buttery, creamy flesh defines the best in a pear. Its sweet flavor comes out when the pear is ripe and juicy. Look for skins that are not bruised. An intense pear flavor is good with nutty and spicy flavors.

Champagne & Pear Drop

¹/₂oz/1.5cl	cognac
¹/₃oz/1cl	pear purée
¹/₃oz/1cl	Passoa liqueur
¹/₃oz/1cl	chamomile syrup
	champagne

GARNISH stem of red currants

 Shake all ingredients, except champagne, with ice. Strain into a chilled champagne flute. Top up with champagne. Stir. Add the garnish on the rim.

Jo-Jo Sling

2oz/6cl	gin
³/₄oz/2.5cl	fresh lemon juice
³/₄oz/2.5cl	pear juice
³/₄oz/2.5cl	apple juice
2 barspoons	vanilla sugar
4 slices	pear
4	white grapes

 Place all ingredients into a blender with ice cubes. Blend quickly. Pour into a tall wine glass with ice. Serve with a straw.

Pearadise Martini

1²/₃oz/5cl	gin
²/₃oz/2cl	pear liqueur
1oz/3cl	pear purée
dash	fresh lemon juice

GARNISH slice of pear

 Shake all ingredients vigorously. Strain into a chilled cocktail glass. Add the garnish on the rim.

Peartini

$1^2/_3$oz/5cl	pear vodka	
$^1/_3$oz/1cl	amaretto liqueur	
$^1/_3$oz/1cl	gomme syrup	
$^2/_3$oz/2cl	fresh lemon juice	

GARNISH fan of pear slices

Shake all ingredients with ice.
Strain into a chilled cocktail glass.
Garnish with a fan of pear slices
(see page 25 on how to make a fan)
on the rim of the glass.

Tuscan Pear

$1^2/_3$oz/5cl	pear vodka
$^1/_2$oz/1.5cl	limoncello
$^1/_2$oz/1.5cl	ginger liqueur
$^1/_3$oz/1cl	gomme syrup
$^2/_3$oz/2cl	orange juice

GARNISH mint tip, dried slice of pear

Shake all ingredients with ice.
Strain into a chilled cocktail glass.
Add the garnish.

Tutti Frutti

1oz/3cl	pear vodka
$^1/_3$oz/1cl	fresh lemon juice
1 tsp	superfine (caster) sugar
$^2/_3$oz/2cl	pear purée
1 bottle	prosecco (Italian sparkling wine)

GARNISH crystallized ginger

Shake all ingredients, except
prosecco, with ice. Strain into a
champagne flute. Top up with
prosecco. Stir until the mixture is
well combined. Add the garnish.

Woody au Pear

$1^1/_3$oz/4cl	bourbon
$^3/_4$oz/2.5cl	Poire William liqueur
$1^3/_4$oz/5cl	pear purée

GARNISH pear spiral, cinnamon stick

Shake all ingredients with ice.
Strain into an old-fashioned glass
filled with ice. Add the garnish.

pineapple

With sweet, juicy, and fragrant flesh under a hard and prickly skin, the rough-leafed varieties are small, and have deep gold flesh, which is better for juice than the less-sweet, larger varieties.

Caramello Colada

2oz/6cl	golden rum
2/3oz/2cl	coconut cream
2/3oz/2cl	fresh lemon juice
3oz/9cl	pineapple juice
2/3oz/2cl	caramel syrup

 Blend all ingredients with crushed ice until smooth. Pour into a chilled cocktail glass. Add the garnish on a cocktail stick across the glass.

GARNISH thin slice of pineapple, maraschino cherry

El Cerro

1 3/4oz/2.5cl	light rum
1 3/4oz/2.5cl	dark rum
1/2oz/1.5	orange curaçao
1/2oz/1.5cl	Galliano liqueur
1 1/3oz/10cl	pineapple juice
dash	grenadine

 Prepare a highball with a sugar crust. Shake all ingredients with ice until well combined. Strain into the highball. Slice the strawberry in half, then drop it and the wedge of pineapple in the drink.

GARNISH wedge of pineapple, strawberry

Pineapple Dream

1 2/3oz/5cl	vodka
1/3oz/1cl	pineapple syrup
1/2 slice	fresh pineapple, diced
2/3oz/2cl	fresh lime juice
dash	egg white

 Muddle the pineapple, syrup, and lime juice in the bottom of a shaker. Add the vodka and ice. Shake. Strain into an old-fashioned glass filled with crushed ice. Add the garnish. Serve with a straw.

GARNISH small wedge of pineapple

Pineapple Margarita

2oz/6cl	añejo (aged) tequila
half	thick slice fresh pineapple
dash	pineapple juice
dash	agave syrup

GARNISH pineapple leaf

Dice the pineapple and add it, with the syrup, to a shaker. Muddle. Add ice and remaining ingredients. Shake. Double strain into a chilled cocktail glass. Cut a slit in the pineapple leaf garnish and place it on the rim.

Playboy II

1²/₃oz/5cl	aged rum
1oz/3cl	pineapple juice
¹/₂oz/1.5cl	cherry liqueur
dash	fresh lime juice

GARNISH delicate small orchid

Shake all ingredients with ice. Strain into a chilled cocktail glass. Add the flower to the glass, and your telephone number on a cocktail coaster.

Shaolin Master

1oz/3cl	VSOP cognac
1oz/3cl	dark rum
¹/₂oz/1.5cl	fresh lemon juice
2oz/6cl	pineapple juice
dash	nutmeg syrup

GARNISH wedge of pineapple, maraschino cherry

Shake all ingredients with ice. Strain into an old-fashioned glass filled with ice. Add the garnish.

Virgin Colada *nonalcoholic

1²/₃oz/8cl	pineapple juice
1oz/3cl	coconut cream
¹/₂oz/1.5cl	heavy (double) cream

GARNISH physalis

Blend all ingredients until smooth. Add a small scoop of crushed ice, then blend again. Pour into a goblet. Add the garnish on the rim. Serve with a straw.

plum

Some plum brandy is made in Mirabelle, France, but the best known of all of the plum brandies is slivovitz, which is made from the small blue Sljiva plum common throughout Eastern Europe and the Balkans.

Baby Fingers

1oz/3cl	sloe gin
1²/₃oz/5cl	gin
2 dashes	Angostura bitters

Shake all ingredients with ice. Strain into a chilled cocktail glass.

Blackthorn

1oz/3cl	sweet vermouth
1¹/₂oz/4.5cl	sloe gin

GARNISH twist of lemon

Stir the sloe gin and vermouth in a mixing glass with ice. Strain into a chilled cocktail glass. Add the garnish in the drink.

Brave Love

2oz/6cl	sloe gin
dash	fresh lemon juice
dash	raspberry juice
	pasteurized egg white

Shake ingredients in a cocktail shaker with ice. Strain into a chilled cocktail glass.

Dark Side

1	peeled dark plum
1oz/3cl	añejo (aged) tequila
1oz/3cl	fresh lime juice
1/2oz/1.5cl	Grand Marnier

Muddle the peeled plum in the bottom of a shaker. Add remaining ingredients and ice. Shake. Strain into a chilled cocktail glass.

Deep Plum

1 1/2oz/4.5cl	plum brandy
1/2oz/1.5cl	fresh lemon juice
1/2oz/1.5cl	orange juice
dash	maraschino liqueur

Shake all ingredients with ice. Strain into a chilled cocktail glass.

Fifty Casino Cocktail

1 1/2oz/4.5cl	gin
1/2oz/1.5cl	plum brandy
1/2oz/1.5cl	sweet vermouth
dash	Cointreau
dash	orange bitters

Stir ingredients in a mixing glass with ice. Strain into a chilled cocktail glass.

Trade Wind

2oz/6cl	golden rum
1/2oz/1.5cl	fresh lime juice
1/2oz/1.5cl	plum brandy
barspoon	gomme syrup

Shake all ingredients with ice. Strain into a chilled cocktail glass.

pomegranate

The seeds in a fresh pomegranate have to be blended then strained in order to make fresh pomegranate juice. The effort is well worth it, since the resulting juice will be a fine balance between sweet and tart. There are also a few top quality brands available to save you the trouble.

Demon Martini

1²/₃oz/5cl	gin
¹/₂oz/1.5cl	white Kina Lillet
quarter	fresh pomegranate
2	thin slices of sweet chili

GARNISH thin slice of chili

Crust half of the rim of a chilled cocktail glass with sugar. Muddle the pomegranate in the bottom of a shaker. Add ice and remaining ingredients. Shake. Strain into the glass. Add the garnish on the rim.

Dolce Vita

1oz/3cl	lemon vodka
²/₃oz/2cl	pomegranate juice
¹/₂oz/1.5cl	pink grapefruit juice
¹/₂oz/1.5cl	Campari
1 barspoon	fresh lime juice
1 barspoon	passion fruit syrup

GARNISH twist of grapefruit

Shake all ingredients with ice. Strain into a chilled cocktail glass. Add the garnish in the drink.

A **Demon Martini** fills the mouth with pomegranate flavor as soon as you take a sip.

Pomegrita

SERVES 6

6oz/18cl	gin
juice	6 pomegranates
4 Tbsp	superfine (caster) sugar

Squeeze the juice from the pomegranates and pass it through a strainer. Pour the juice, gin, and sugar in a bowl and stir to dissolve the sugar. Freeze the bowl overnight. When ready to serve, use a spoon to break up the mixture. Serve in shot glasses with a teaspoon on the side.

Pome Heights

1oz/3cl	light rum
1oz/3cl	dark rum
^{1}/2oz/1.5cl	coconut rum
1^{2}/3oz/5cl	fresh pomegranate juice
2oz/6cl	pineapple juice
1oz/3cl	gomme syrup

GARNISH slice of pineapple, maraschino cherry

Shake all ingredients with ice. Strain into a highball filled with crushed ice. Add the garnish. Serve with a straw.

Pomegranate Julep

1^{2}/3 oz/5cl	vodka
1oz/3cl	fresh pomegranate juice
1oz/3cl	grapefruit juice
^{1}/2oz/1.5cl	honey syrup
4	mint leaves

GARNISH sprig of mint

Bruise the four mint leaves with the honey syrup in a mixing glass. Add to a shaker with the remaining ingredients. Shake. Strain into an old-fashioned glass filled with ice. Add the garnish.

Pomegranny

1^{3}/4oz/5cl	gin
1^{3}/4oz/5cl	fresh pomegranate juice
4oz/12cl	bitter lemon

GARNISH slice of cucumber

Pour the ingredients over ice in a highball glass. Add the garnish on the rim of the glass.

Pome-tini

1²/₃oz/5cl	vodka
1oz/3cl	fresh pomegranate juice
¹/₂oz/1.5cl	fresh lime juice
¹/₂oz/1.5cl	gomme syrup

Shake all ingredients with ice. Strain into a chilled cocktail glass. Add the garnish on the rim of the glass and let it trail down.

GARNISH orange spiral

Pomiri

1²/₃oz/5cl	light rum
1oz/3cl	fresh pomegranate juice
¹/₂oz/1.5cl	maraschino liqueur
1oz/3cl	fresh lime juice
¹/₂oz/1.5cl	gomme syrup

Shake all ingredients with ice. Strain into a highball filled with ice. Add the wedge of lime.

GARNISH wedge of lime

Strike Out

1¹/₂oz/4.5cl	vodka
splash	Pernod or ouzo
1 Tbsp	Cointreau
1¹/₂ Tbsp	fresh lime juice
1oz/3cl	pomegranate juice

Splash some Pernod in a chilled cocktail glass, swirl it around, and then discard it from the glass. Shake all ingredients with ice. Strain into a chilled cocktail glass.

Wonderful Wild Berries

2oz/6cl	wild berries vodka
1oz/3cl	pomegranate juice
¹/₂oz/1.5cl	fresh lime juice
	club soda

Shake the vodka and juice with ice. Strain into a highball filled with ice. Top up with soda. Stir. Squeeze the lime into the drink.

GARNISH wedge of lime

raspberry

Tart flavors dominate in a fresh red raspberry so it's best to use raspberry juice with other flavors that will not compete with it, such as chocolate, vanilla, rose water, and lavender. Crème de framboise and fresh raspberries is a luxurious combination.

Caveman Crush

$^1/_3$oz/1cl	**Plymouth damson gin**
6	**fresh raspberries**
$^3/_4$oz/2.5cl	**fresh lemon juice**
$^1/_3$oz/1cl	**clear honey**
$^1/_3$oz/1cl	**raspberry liqueur**
1oz/3cl	**Scotch**
	ginger beer

GARNISH sprig of mint, raspberry

Shake all ingredients, except the ginger beer, with ice. Strain into a highball filled with crushed ice. Top up with ginger beer. Garnish with a sprig of mint and a raspberry. Serve with a straw.

Coutts

1$^1/_3$oz/4cl	**vodka**
$^2/_3$oz/2cl	**cold tea**
$^2/_3$oz/2cl	**raspberry purée**
$^1/_3$oz/1cl	**Bénédictine**
$^1/_3$oz/1cl	**fresh lime juice**
2 tsps	**honey**

GARNISH sprig of mint, raspberry

Shake all ingredients with ice. Strain into a chilled cocktail glass. Add the garnish on a toothpick on the edge of the glass.

Raspberry Collins

1²/₃oz/5cl	raspberry vodka
¹/₂oz/1.5cl	Chambord liqueur
¹/₂oz/1.5cl	fresh lemon juice
7	fresh raspberries
¹/₃oz/1cl	gomme syrup
	club soda

 Muddle the raspberries with the gomme in the bottom of a shaker. Add ice and remaining ingredients except the club soda. Shake well. Strain into a highball filled with ice. Top up with soda. Stir. Add the garnish on top of the drink.

Scotch Club

1³/₄oz/5cl	12-year-old Scotch
²/₃oz/2cl	raspberry liqueur
¹/₂oz/1.5cl	fresh lemon juice
¹/₂oz/1.5cl	pasteurized egg white
2	fresh raspberries

GARNISH 2 fresh raspberries

 Shake all ingredients with ice. Strain into a chilled cocktail glass. Place the raspberry garnish on top of the frothy drink.

strawberry

A flavor burst enters the mouth at the bite of a fresh, ripe, sweet strawberry. A summer fruit (although you can buy them year round) the strawberry has a subtle fragrance on the nose. Crème de fraise is slightly thicker than regular strawberry liqueur.

Berry Burst

1oz/3cl	vodka
1/2oz/1.5cl	crème de cassis
3	fresh strawberries
6	fresh blueberries
5oz/15cl	7Up

Muddle the cassis and fruit in the bottom of a shaker. Add ice and the vodka. Shake well. Strain into a highball glass. Top up with 7Up. Stir.

Coccinella

2/3oz/2cl	gin
1oz/3cl	Campari
two	large strawberries
dash	superfine (caster) sugar

GARNISH eight Szechuan peppercorns

Muddle the strawberries and sugar in a shaker. Add ice, gin, and the Campari. Shake well. Strain into a chilled cocktail glass. Garnish with the peppercorns.

Franklin Cobbler

1²/3oz/5cl	bourbon
quarter	slice orange
2	mint leaves
2	strawberries
2/3oz/2cl	crème de fraise
dash	gomme syrup

GARNISH quarter slice of orange, mint tip, half strawberry

Gently muddle the slice of orange, mint leaves, and strawberries in a large old-fashioned glass. Add the remaining ingredients and fill the glass with crushed ice. Stir vigorously. Add the garnish.

Strawberry Jive

1²/₃oz/5cl	gin
2	basil leaves
3	strawberries
2	mint leaves
²/₃oz/2cl	gomme syrup
2 dashes	fresh lemon juice
1oz/3cl	fresh orange juice

GARNISH half a strawberry, sprig of mint

Muddle the mint, strawberries, and basil leaves in the bottom of a shaker, along with the syrup. Add the remaining ingredients and ice. Shake. Strain into an old-fashioned glass filled with ice. Add the garnish on the rim.

Strawberry Margarita

1²/₃oz/5cl	silver tequila
¹/₂oz/2cl	strawberry liqueur
¹/₂oz/1.5cl	fresh lime juice
handful	strawberries

GARNISH strawberry, sprig of mint

Blend all ingredients with crushed ice. Pour into a Margarita glass. Add the garnish on the side.

Strawberry Spice

2oz/6cl	cachaça
3	strawberries, diced
1 tsp	superfine (caster) sugar
2 dashes	ground cinnamon

GARNISH cinnamon stick, slice of strawberry

Muddle the strawberries, sugar, and cinnamon in the bottom of a shaker. Add ice and the cachaça. Shake. Strain into an old-fashioned glass filled with ice. Add the cinnamon stick in the drink, topped by the strawberry.

Tropical Butterfly

1²/₃oz/5cl	gin
1²/₃oz/5cl	passion fruit juice
¹/₃oz/1cl	elderflower cordial
¹/₂oz/1.5cl	pear purée
3 to 4	fresh strawberries

GARNISH strawberry

Muddle the strawberries in the bottom of the shaker. Add ice and the remaining ingredients. Shake. Strain into a highball filled with ice. Add the garnish on the rim.

tomato

Sweet-acid tomato flavors abound in farmer's market produce as opposed to supermarket types. Look for plump tomatoes with a shiny skin, that give slightly when touched, and are free from bruising. If making tomato juice, strain the juiced matter through a piece of muslin to ensure the seeds are gone.

Bloody Bull

1oz/3cl	vodka
2oz/6cl	beef bouillon or
	condensed consommé
2oz/6cl	tomato juice
dash	fresh lemon juice
2 dashes	Worcestershire sauce
pinch	celery salt

 Shake all ingredients with ice. Strain into a highball filled with ice.

Bloody Mary

1²/₃oz/5cl	vodka
5oz/15cl	tomato juice
²/₃oz/2cl	fresh lemon juice
pinch	celery salt
2 dashes	Worcestershire sauce
2 dashes	Tabasco sauce
	ground black pepper

GARNISH wedge of lime, celery stalk (optional)

Fill a highball with ice cubes. Pour the tomato and lemon juices into the glass, then the vodka. Stir. Add the spices. Stir. Add a quick twist of black pepper. Add the wedge of lime on the rim, and a stalk of celery if requested. Serve with a stirrer.

Vampiro

1²/₃oz/5cl	silver tequila
2¹/₃oz/7cl	tomato juice
³/₄oz/2.5cl	fresh orange juice
1 tsp	clear honey
¹/₃oz/1cl	fresh lime juice
half slice	onion, finely chopped
few slices	red hot chili
few dashes	Worcestershire sauce
	salt

GARNISH wedge of lime

Pour ingredients, starting with the juices and then the tequila, into a shaker with ice. Shake. Strain into a highball filled with ice. Garnish with a wedge of lime sitting on the rim of the glass and a slice of red chili adjacent it.

Virgin Mary   *nonalcoholic

3¹/₃oz/10cl	tomato juice
²/₃oz/2cl	fresh lemon juice
2 dashes	Worcestershire sauce
dash	Tabasco sauce
pinch	celery salt

GARNISH wedge of lime, ground black pepper

Pour all ingredients one at a time into a highball filled with ice. Stir well. Add the garnish. Sprinkle freshly ground black pepper over the drink.

watermelon

In a section of its own because of its delightful color and flavor, this large green-skinned fruit has a sweet taste and has a watery juice that lends itself to cocktail recipes.

Vanilla Melon Fizz

1oz/3cl	vodka
1oz/3cl	Galliano
²/₃oz/2cl	fresh lemon juice
1 tsp	vanilla sugar
1 tsp	fresh grated coconut
dash	gomme syrup
2 cubes	watermelon

Muddle the watermelon and the coconut in the bottom of the shaker with the sugar. Add ice and the remaining ingredients. Shake. Double strain into an old-fashioned glass filled with ice.

Watermelon Martini

1²/₃oz/5cl	vodka
wedge	watermelon
dash	gomme syrup

GARNISH small wedge of watermelon

Muddle the watermelon in the bottom of a shaker. Add ice and ingredients. Shake. Double strain into a cocktail glass. Add the garnish on the rim.

Watermelon Sombrero

1²/₃oz/5cl	silver tequila
¹/₂oz/1.5cl	fresh lime juice
¹/₂oz/1.5cl	agave syrup
5 cubes	watermelon, diced
¹/₂oz/1.5cl	Cointreau

GARNISH wedge of watermelon

Gently muddle the melon in the bottom of a shaker. Add ice and the remaining ingredients. Shake. Double strain into a chilled cocktail glass. Add the garnish on the rim.

Watermelon Martini is a refreshing take on the classic martini-style cocktail.

herbs

infusing

Creating an infused flavor is a creative process, one
that's been carried out for centuries. All infused
spirits and liqueurs are produced using the same
basic method: an ingredient is steeped in alcohol
for a long time, during which the flavor of the
ingredient is fused into the spirit.

Infusions can be made at home or in the professional bar. All you need is the essential part of a fresh herb, a bottle of the selected spirit, a cool, dark cupboard space, and patience.

Any alcohol can be infused, including vodka, brandy, kirsch, tequila, and rum. You can also infuse schnapps with plum, pear, cherry, apricot, and orange peel, to name but a few of the fruits capable of bringing a rich flavor to a spirit. As a sweetener for some liqueurs, you can use a homemade simple sugar syrup, or bottled gomme syrup.

The combinations of spirit and ingredient are endless, as is the depth of flavor you can achieve. If, at the end of the time you thought it would take to infuse you find the flavor not as strong as you wanted, leave the mixture for a week or two more. On the other hand, if the flavor is too strong, then add more spirit until the taste is the strength you like.

You can buy premixed vodkas in many flavors, but a homemade infusion will taste entirely different, especially when you have managed to get the process down to a fine art.

Now, bartenders around the globe are making their own unique infusions, using stems of rosemary and lavender, leaves of basil and sage, entire chilis, cinnamon sticks, delicate petals from a rose or two, rind from citrus fruits … all in search of that undiscovered flavor.

When used in cocktails, you will be surprised at the unexpected layers of flavor in the drink. **Good luck!**

basil

Known to be good for the mind, basil imparts a deliciously aromatic flavor to a cocktail. The usual basil flavor is bright green, sweet, with a slight hint of licorice.

Basil Martini

2oz/6cl	basil vodka
$^1/_2$oz/1.5cl	dry vermouth
3 leaves	fresh basil
dash	gomme syrup

GARNISH basil leaf

Shake all ingredients with ice. Strain into a chilled cocktail glass. Add the garnish on top of the drink.

Euphoria Cocktail

1$^2/_3$oz/5cl	basil vodka
$^1/_2$oz/1.5cl	wild strawberry liqueur
$^1/_2$oz/1.5cl	Parfait Amour
dash	fresh lemon juice
2 leaves	fresh purple basil

GARNISH purple basil leaf sprayed very lightly with CK Euphoria for Men

Shake all ingredients well with ice. Double strain into a chilled cocktail glass. Add the garnish on top of the drink. This gives an incredible aroma to the drink.

Oriental Tea Party

2oz/6cl	vodka
1oz/3cl	apple juice
$^1/_2$oz/1.5cl	fresh lime juice
$^1/_2$oz/1.5cl	cranberry juice
4	basil leaves

GARNISH thin wedge of apple, basil leaf

Shake all ingredients with ice. Strain into an old-fashioned glass filled with ice. Add the garnish.

bénédictine

An old, herbal remedy that became a popular after-dinner drink, Bénédictine is made from 27 plants and spices. It has a honey flavor with hints of medicinal bitter herb and orange flavors.

B & B

1oz/3cl	brandy
1oz/3cl	Bénédictine

 Pour ingredients into a brandy glass. Stir.

Bobby Burns

2oz/6cl	Scotch whisky
1oz/3cl	Bénédictine
1/2oz/1.5cl	red vermouth

GARNISH twist of orange

 Pour all ingredients into a mixing glass with ice. Stir. Strain into a chilled cocktail glass. Add the garnish in the drink.

Brainstorm

1²/₃oz/5cl	bourbon
1oz/3cl	Bénédictine
1/2oz/1.5cl	dry vermouth

GARNISH twist of lemon

Pour all ingredients into a mixing glass with ice. Stir. Strain into a chilled cocktail glass. Add the garnish in the drink.

cilantro [coriander]

An herb of the parsley family, cilantro has a pungent flavor, with a faint undertone of anise. It has a piquant citrus-flavored, biting tang. Be sure you don't pick up flat-leaf parsley, which looks similar to cilantro when on the shelf.

Deep Thinker

1²/₃oz/5cl	spiced rum
1	lime, diced
6 sprigs	cilantro
1¹/₂ tsp	demerara sugar
¹/₂oz/1.5cl	elderflower cordial

Muddle the lime, cilantro, and sugar in an old-fashioned glass.
Add crushed ice and remaining ingredients. Stir well.

Limeade

2oz/6cl	Licor 43
1oz/3cl	vanilla syrup
handful	fresh cilantro
1oz/3cl	fresh lime juice

GARNISH wedge of lime

Muddle the cilantro with the vanilla syrup in an old-fashioned glass.
Add the lime juice. Fill the glass with crushed ice. Add the Licor 43. Stir. Add more crushed ice, then add the garnish.

Mellow Yellow

2oz/6cl	gin
²/₃oz/2cl	limoncello
¹/₃oz/1cl	fresh lemon juice
4 to 5	fresh cilantro leaves
	lemon sorbet

GARNISH sprig of cilantro

Shake all ingredients with ice.
Strain into a champagne coupe over a scoop of lemon sorbet. Add the sprig of cilantro.

elderflower

The cordial made from this flower has a delicate, scented taste. In liqueur form, it has Riesling and Muscat grape aromas; after that, some gooseberry and green plum notes emerge with intense and beguiling flavors of tangerine, tropical fruit, and persimmon.

Elderflower Fizz

2oz/6cl	brandy
1/2oz/1.5cl	elderflower cordial
	7Up

GARNISH wedge of lemon

Shake the brandy and cordial with ice. Strain into a highball filled with ice. Top up with 7Up. Add the garnish in the drink.

Elderflower Margarita

1²/3oz/5cl	silver tequila
²/3oz/2cl	elderflower cordial
2/3oz/2 cl	apple juice
1/2oz/1.5cl	fresh lime juice

GARNISH wedge of lime

Shake all ingredients with ice. Strain into a chilled cocktail glass. Add the garnish on the rim.

Sal's St. Germain

1²/3oz/5cl	St. Germain elderflower liqueur
1/2oz/1.5cl	fresh lemon juice
1/2oz/1.5cl	orange juice
dash	Peychaud's orange bitters
dash	pasteurized egg white

GARNISH elderflower blossom

Shake all ingredients well with ice. Strain into an old-fashioned glass with ice. Add the garnish on top of the drink.

lavender

The taste of lavender is delicate, subtly spicy and warm. Be sure the lavender buds you use are organic, or at least unsprayed. It adds piquancy to a cocktail.

Lavenderita

1¹/₃oz/4cl	tequila
1	fresh lavender bud
¹/₂oz/1.5cl	Parfait Amour
1 tsp	peach liqueur
2 tsp	gomme syrup

GARNISH stem of lavender

 Muddle the lavender bud in the bottom of a shaker. Add remaining ingredients, and ice. Shake well. Double strain into a chilled cocktail glass. Add the lavender on top of the drink.

Lavender-ini

1oz/3cl	vanilla vodka
2oz/6cl	lavender-infused vodka
dash	fresh lemon juice
2 dashes	gomme syrup

GARNISH stem of lavender

 Shake all ingredients with ice. Strain into a chilled cocktail glass. Add the garnish.

Lavender Mojito

2oz/6cl	Charbay rum or vanilla bean rum
1oz/3cl	fresh lime juice
1oz/3cl	gomme syrup
3 buds	lavender
5	mint leaves
	club soda

GARNISH long-stemmed lavender bud

In a mixing glass, muddle the mint and the lavender with the lime juice and syrup. Add ice, then the rum and stir. Pour into a highball filled with ice. Top up with club soda. Stir. Add the bud into the drink so the tip shows at the top.

lemongrass

An Asian cookery ingredient, the pale-looking lemongrass has segued into the cocktail bar. It has a light lemon flavor, as its name suggests. Buy it as fresh as you can.

Cancun Cooler

2oz/6cl	añejo (aged) tequila
1oz/3cl	fresh lemon juice
¹/₂oz/1.5cl	coconut syrup
1oz/3cl	apple juice
1oz/3cl	pineapple juice
2in/5cm	piece lemongrass, chopped
	ginger ale

GARNISH wedge of lime, lemongrass stalk

Muddle the lemongrass in a shaker. Add remaining ingredients, except ginger ale. Add ice. Shake well. Double strain into a highball filled with ice. Top up with ginger ale. Stir. Add the lime on the rim and the stalk across the drink.

Rogue Lemongrass

1 blade	lemongrass, ³/₄in/1.5cm long
3 sprigs	cilantro leaves
2oz/6cl	vanilla vodka
²/₃oz/2cl	gomme syrup
1oz/3cl	fresh grapefruit juice
2 drops	orange bitters

Push the inner rolls of lemongrass out with a barspoon to make a straw. Slice the inner rolls and place them in a shaker with the cilantro leaves. Muddle well. Add the remaining ingredients. Add ice and shake well. Double strain into a chilled cocktail glass.

mint

There are a few flavors of mint, but the most common is the refreshing spearmint. When buying fresh mint, look for perky, bright green leaves with no signs of wilting.

Kentucky Derby Cooler

1²/3oz/5cl	bourbon
small sprig	mint leaves
3oz/9cl	strong breakfast tea
²/3oz/2cl	maple syrup
1	lemon wedge
1	large orange wedge

GARNISH sprig of mint

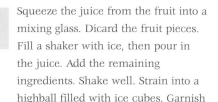

Squeeze the juice from the fruit into a mixing glass. Dicard the fruit pieces. Fill a shaker with ice, then pour in the juice. Add the remaining ingredients. Shake well. Strain into a highball filled with ice cubes. Garnish with the sprig of mint.

Mint Julep

1²/3oz/5cl	bourbon
bunch	fresh mint leaves
1 tsp	superfine (caster) sugar
1 tsp	cold water
	club soda

GARNISH sprig of mint

Place the mint in an old-fashioned glass. Add the sugar and water. Muddle until the sugar is dissolved. Add the bourbon. Fill the glass with crushed ice. Stir. Add the garnish. Serve with a straw and a stirrer.

Mojito

1³/₄oz/5cl	light rum
1 tsp	superfine (caster) sugar
²/₃oz/2cl	fresh lime juice
sprig	fresh mint
	sparkling water

Put the sugar and lime juice in the bottom of a highball with a heavy base. Add the mint leaves and muddle with the end of a barspoon or a wooden muddler to release the essence from the mint. Add the rum and fill the glass with crushed ice. Top up with sparkling water. Stir. Serve with a stirrer.

oregano

A strong and gutsy herbal flavor, oregano goes well with lemon. It has a mild peppery bite to it, which comes through even when the herb is combined with many other flavors.

Scubarello

1²/₃oz/5cl	vodka
1 stem	fresh oregano
3	raspberries
3	blackberries
1 tsp	demerara sugar
²/₃oz/2cl	fresh lime juice
¹/₃oz/1cl	crème de framboise
¹/₂oz/1.5cl	crème de mûre
	club soda

Muddle the berries with the sugar and oregano in the bottom of a shaker. Add ice and remaining ingredients, except soda. Shake well. Strain into a highball filled with ice. Top up with soda.

GARNISH raspberry, blackberry, tip of oregano

rosemary

A familiar herb, rosemary presents the taste buds with a woodsy flavor with a hint of pine. It is mintlike yet sweeter, with a slight ginger finish. It is good in a cocktail when used as a subtle accent.

Rosa Maria

2oz/6cl	silver tequila
1/2oz/1.5cl	Cointreau
1oz/3cl	fresh lime juice
1oz/3cl	agave syrup
bunch	fresh rosemary

GARNISH sprig of rosemary

Muddle the rosemary and the syrup in the bottom of a shaker. Add remaining ingredients. Shake well to combine the flavors. Double strain into a chilled cocktail glass. Add the garnish in the drink.

Rosemary Cooler

2oz/6cl	vodka
1/2oz/1.5cl	mango syrup
1/2oz/1.5cl	fresh lime juice
1 1/3oz/4cl	blood orange juice
dash	grenadine
sprig	fresh rosemary

GARNISH sprig of rosemary, wedge of orange

Muddle the rosemary in the bottom of the shaker. Add the remaining ingredients. Shake with ice. Strain into a highball filled with crushed ice. Add the garnish.

Rosemary-tini

2oz/6cl	rosemary-infused vodka
1/2oz/1.5cl	dry vermouth
dash	Pernod

GARNISH sprig of rosemary

Shake all ingredients with ice. Strain into a chilled cocktail glass. Add the garnish.

The star of **Rosemary Cooler** is the long sprig of rosemary, which adds even more flavor.

sage

Its soft green-gray leaves are big and flat, and easy to cut or chop.
When touched, the plant releases a woody, earthy scent into the air.

Sage Fan

1²/₃oz/5cl	vodka
²/₃oz/2cl	limoncello
1oz/3cl	apple juice
3 leaves	fresh sage
dash	honey syrup
dash	fresh lemon juice

GARNISH fan of apple, sage leaves

Break the sage leaves into segments and place in a shaker. Add ice and the remaining ingredients. Shake. Strain into an old-fashioned glass filled with ice. Add the fan of apple with the sage leaves inserted in the middle of it. Serve with a straw.

Sage Love

1²/₃oz/5cl	light rum
²/₃oz/2cl	mandarin liqueur
¹/₂oz/1.5cl	fresh lime juice
1²/₃oz/5cl	pineapple juice
1²/₃oz/5cl	passion fruit juice
4	leaves fresh sage

GARNISH sage leaves

Break the sage leaves into segments and place in a shaker. Add ice and the remaining ingredients. Shake. Double strain into a highball filled with crushed ice. Add the garnish on top. Serve with a straw.

Wisely Yours

12/3oz/5cl	añejo (aged) tequila
1/3oz/1cl	white crème de cacao
1/2oz/1.5cl	amaretto
1oz/3cl	orange juice
2	kumquats

GARNISH sage leaves

Break the sage leaves into segments and place in a shaker. Add ice and the remaining ingredients. Shake. Double strain into a chilled cocktail glass. Add the garnish on top.

thyme

The flavor has been described as tasting delicately green with a faint clove aftertaste. Lemon thyme is delicate and, like all other thyme flavors, is extra pungent when fresh.

Evening Thyme

1oz/3cl	vodka
2/3oz/2cl	Lillet Rouge
1/3oz/1cl	triple sec
2 dashes	Angostura bitters
sprig	thyme

GARNISH sprig of thyme

 Shake all ingredients with ice. Double strain into a chilled cocktail glass. Add the garnish.

Perfect Thyme

2¹/₂oz/6.5cl	gin
few	small slices fresh ginger
few slices	lemongrass stalk
sprig	fresh thyme

 Muddle the ginger, lemongrass, and thyme in a mixing glass. Add ice cubes, then the gin. Stir to combine all flavors. Strain into a chilled cocktail glass.

Spring Thyme

1oz/3cl	citrus vodka
1oz/3cl	green apple purée
1oz/3cl	limoncello
1oz/3cl	thyme syrup
1oz/3cl	fresh lime juice

GARNISH sprig of thyme

 See page 30 for how to make thyme syrup. Shake all ingredients with ice. Strain into a chilled cocktail glass. Add the garnish across the top of the drink.

nut flavors

The world of flavor would be less interesting if there were no subtle nut flavors. Take the almond, for example. There are two kinds of almonds: the bitter almond from Asia and the Mediterranean region, and the sweet almond, of which more than 100 varieties are grown in California alone.

Drinkers of amaretto, considered by some to be the king of nut-flavored liqueurs, will already know its flavor is defined by the bitter almonds with which it is made. You can also taste almond in a crème de noyau, which is a red-colored liqueur made from almond pits, and sometimes with peach or apricot pits. Pink in color, it is a fine alternative to amaretto. Almond nuts are also good for you because they are strong in vitamin E, so perhaps use slivers as a garnish.

From the Piedmont region of Italy, Frangelico liqueur is made with toasted wild hazelnuts, combined with cocoa and vanilla berries, rhubarb root, and sweet orange flowers plus other natural flavors. Add to this an infusion of alcohol, then a period in fine oak casks to mature, and you have a golden, smooth liqueur that is especially tasty. You can serve it straight, chilled, over ice, in a cocktail, or mixed with tonic or club soda.

A walnut is used in crème de noix, a liqueur prized for its slightly sweet flavor. It also boasts the addition of honey and is sometimes called eau-de-vie de noix.

However, the everlasting appeal of a nut-flavored liqueur lies in the sweet, full-bodied flavor, mellow in the mouth, with an interesting, lingering aftertaste.

They are great mixers in after-dinner cocktails, and if that's your taste, then you'll be nuts about these recipes.

almond

When combined with other ingredients, the nutty almond flavor comes through on the finish. Light and slightly sweet, this is an intriguing but not a strong flavor.

Mai Tai

2oz/6cl	**aged rum**
²/₃oz/2cl	**orange curaçao**
²/₃oz/2cl	**fresh lime juice**
²/₃oz/2cl	**orgeat**

GARNISH wedge of lime, sprig of mint

Shake all ingredients with ice. Strain into an old-fashioned glass filled with ice. Add the garnish on a cocktail stick.

Tara Special

²/₃oz/2cl	**amaretto**
²/₃oz/2cl	**white peach purée**
3	**raspberries**
1 dash	**fresh orange juice**
	prosecco

GARNISH two raspberries, mint leaf

Shake all ingredients. Strain into a chilled champagne flute. Top up with prosecco. Add the garnish on a cocktail stick.

Tennessee Squirrel

1²/₃oz/5cl	**Jack Daniels**
³/₄oz/2.5cl	**crème de Noyaux**
1	**passion fruit**
²/₃oz/2cl	**fresh lemon juice**
2 dashes	**passion fruit syrup**

GARNISH quarter of passion fruit

Shake all ingredients with ice. Strain into an old-fashioned glass filled with ice cubes. Add the garnish to a cocktail stick and place it across the glass.

Tennessee Squirrel has a delicate passion fruit flavor, while **Va-Va-Voom** shows off an apple fan.

hazelnut

The flavor of toasted hazelnuts fills the mouth when you taste a hazelnut liqueur in a cocktail. It also delivers a full-bodied texture to further enhance the combination.

Fosbury Flip

1²/₃oz/5cl	aged rum
1oz/3cl	Frangelico
¹/₂oz/1.5cl	apricot brandy
2oz/6cl	fresh orange juice
¹/₂oz/1.5cl	fresh lime juice
dash	grenadine
1	fresh egg yolk (pasteurized)

GARNISH grated orange zest

Shake all ingredients with ice. Strain into a highball filled with ice. Add the garnish over the top of the cocktail.

Frenzy

1oz/3cl	hazelnut liqueur
¹/₂oz/1.5cl	Aperol
1oz/3cl	limoncello
¹/₂oz/1.5cl	fresh lemon juice

Shake all ingredients with ice. Strain into an old-fashioned glass filled with ice.

Hazelnut-ini

2oz/6cl	vodka
²/₃oz/2cl	Frangelico
dash	white crème de cacao

GARNISH orange spiral

Shake all ingredients with ice. Strain into a chilled cocktail glass. Add the orange spiral.

Hazelnut flavor dominates in this **Hazelnut-ini** that is enhanced by a lemon spiral garnish.

spices

chili
cinnamon
ginger
pepper
saffron
vanilla

As you can see from the image of the Spicy Fifty cocktail on page 2, the small red hot chili is one of my favorite spices. It not only looks exotic on the rim of a glass, it also delivers the hot and spicy flavor needed to wake up the mouth.

However, not all chilis are piercingly hot. I like the jalapeño, which is a moderately hot chili, for dicing and muddling, and the bird's eye, which is hotter, for decoration. There are hundreds of types of chili, some hot, some milder. Therefore, if you use the chili listed in the recipes, you will not give your palate too much of a taste surpise.

You can use spices in cocktails as an infusion, or as a fresh spice, muddled or shaken with other ingredients. If you want to make your own spicy infusion, preferably use vodka as the base spirit (see page 130 for more details).

The key to using a spicy flavor is to hint at it, and not overwhelm all else in the mix, so look for balance.

Of the other spices in this section, ginger is one that's perhaps already familiar to drinkers of hot and spicy cocktails, the kind you sip when it is cold. However, fresh ginger has a zingy flavor and pieces of it can be muddled, or used as an infusion, in the range of contemporary and healthy cocktails available in bars today.

Cinnamon sticks are great in hot drinks and for using to infuse the spicy flavor in a spirit. You can also sprinkle grated cinnamon or nutmeg over the top of a creamy cocktail to give a spicy aroma.

There are recipes using ground black pepper, saffron, and vanilla. The idea of saffron as a cocktail ingredient is unusual, but it is a great flavor for mixing with an herb such as tarragon, and an orange curaçao liqueur.

I chose a sweet and spicy combination for a recipe with champagne and honey vodka. The pepper on the nose is tempered with the hint of honey. The vanilla recipes make use of three different forms of vanilla: a vanilla liqueur, a vanilla pod, and vanilla vodka. Each is combined with a variety of fruit and spirits to let the vanilla flavor shine through.

Variety is the spice of life—here's a selection of recipes guaranteed to cause your mouth to tingle as you enjoy the complexity of the combinations.

chili

The flavor of chili ranges from mild to very hot, depending on the type you select. For cocktails, use the smaller bird's eye chili if you can find it, or the usual red chili. The flavor is concentrated at the top of the pod. Chilis are rich in vitamin C and are high in potassium, magnesium, and iron.

Hot Gringo

2oz/6cl	añejo (aged) tequila
1oz/3cl	fresh lime juice
¹/₂oz/1.5cl	lemongrass cordial
3 thin slices	chili

GARNISH wedge of lime

Shake all ingredients with ice. Strain into a chilled cocktail glass. Add the wedge of lime.

Love, Honor, and Obey

1²/₃oz/5cl	vanilla-infused vodka
¹/₃oz/1cl	fresh lime juice
1	lemongrass stalk, diced
3	large pieces fresh watermelon
2 thin slices	bird's eye chili
1 tsp	honey

Muddle the lemongrass, watermelon, chili, and honey in the bottom of a shaker. Add the vodka and the lime juice, and ice. Shake and double strain into a chilled cocktail glass.

Spicy Fifty

1²/₃oz/5cl	vanilla vodka
¹/₂oz/1.5cl	fresh lime juice
¹/₃oz/1cl	honey syrup
¹/₂oz/1.5cl	elderflower cordial
2	thin slices of red chili

GARNISH bird's eye chili

 Shake ingredients and strain into a chilled martini glass. Place a little red chili on the rim of the glass.

Stealth Margarita

2oz/6cl	tequila
1oz/3cl	Grand Marnier
¹/₂oz/1.5cl	elderflower cordial
2 cubes	frozen lemon juice

GARNISH small green chili

 Pour the first three ingredients in a mixing glass with ice. Stir. Place the lemon ice cubes in a chilled cocktail glass. Strain the mixture over it. Split the small chili halfway along its length to expose the seeds and slide it around the rim of the glass to add a hint of chili.

cinnamon

This is the dried bark of laurel trees and has a sweet, woody flavor that is familiar to us in hot teas and buns. It is available in stick form, and as powder.

Big Kiss

1²/₃oz/5cl	vanilla vodka
½oz/1.5cl	crème de noisette
1oz/3cl	Goldschläger cinnamon schnapps
½oz/1.5cl	chilled mineral water

GARNISH cinnamon stick

 Shake all ingredients with ice. Strain into a chilled cocktail glass. Add the garnish across the top of the glass.

Cinnamon May

1½oz/4.5cl	vodka
½oz/1.5cl	cinnamon syrup
½oz/1.5cl	kiwi liqueur
2	kumquats, diced

GARNISH cinnamon stick

 Muddle the kumquat in the bottom of a shaker. Add ice and remaining ingredients. Shake. Double strain into a chilled cocktail glass. Add the garnish in the drink.

Golden Jubilee

1¹/₃oz/4cl	gin
½oz/1.5cl	Goldschläger cinnamon schnapps
½oz/1.5cl	Parfait Amour
	champagne

 Add the gin, Goldschläger, and Parfait Amour to a mixing glass with ice. Strain into a chilled cocktail glass. Top up with champagne.

ginger

I like to use fresh ginger in cocktails because of its sharp and clean flavor. It adds a zing to any drink when used in the right proportion. Young ginger is juicy and fleshy with a mild taste. Its essential oils cause the fragrance.

Ginger Nut

1¹/₃oz/4cl	gin
¹/₂oz/1.5cl	crème de noisette
¹/₂oz/1.5cl	caramel liqueur
1¹/₃oz/4cl	fresh orange juice
1 tsp	fresh ginger (or powdered)
	ginger beer

Shake all ingredients, except ginger beer, with ice. Strain into a highball filled with ice. Top up with ginger beer. Stir.

GARNISH two thin slices of ginger, tip of mint

Hot & Cold Toddy

6oz/18cl	ginger-infused apple cider
thin slice	fresh ginger
2oz/6cl	bourbon

Serve hot: Heat the cider but do not boil. Add the bourbon. Serve in a heatproof glass.

Serve cold: Pour the bourbon and cider mixture into a mixing glass filled with ice. Pour into a highball filled with ice.

Rama

1oz/3cl	tequila
¹/₂oz/1.5cl	mandarin liqueur
¹/₂oz/1.5cl	cranberry juice
¹/₂oz/1.5cl	gomme syrup infused with crushed ginger

Crust half of the glass rim with salt. Shake all ingredients with ice. Strain into a chilled cocktail glass. Add the garnish on the rim.

GARNISH wedge of lime

pepper

This is the King of Spices and is excellent for your digestion. Black peppercorns have the strongest flavor of all the peppercorns. They have a warm aroma and a spicy flavor.

Arabian Dream

1¹/₃oz/4cl	honey vodka
2oz/6cl	fresh apple juice
¹/₂oz/1.5cl	champagne
dash	grenadine
5 twists	black pepper

GARNISH wedge of lime, ground pepper

 Shake all ingredients with ice. Strain into a highball filled with crushed ice. Add the garnish on top of the drink.

Grand Pepper

1³/₄oz/5cl	vodka
²/₃oz/2cl	Grand Marnier
¹/₃oz/1cl	strawberry liqueur
¹/₂ tsp	pink peppercorns

 Shake all ingredients with ice. Strain into a chilled cocktail glass. Crush a few pink peppercorns and sprinkle them over the top.

Pepper Jack

1²/₃oz/5cl	bourbon
²/₃oz/2cl	pepper vodka
1	fresh kiwi fruit, peeled and diced
1	fresh lime, diced
dash	gomme syrup

GARNISH slice of kiwi fruit, sprinkle of fresh ground pepper

 Muddle the flesh of the kiwi with the diced lime and the gomme syrup in a shaker. Add ice, the bourbon, and the vodka. Shake well. Strain into a chilled cocktail glass. Set the kiwi slice on the rim and grind fresh pepper over the drink.

An **Arabian Dream** has spicy pepper on the nose and a lime spiral for visual effect.

saffron

Bright yellow in color, saffron has a strong perfume and a bitter, honeylike taste on the palate. It is pleasantly spicy and can linger on the tongue.

Saffron Dune

1²/₃oz/5cl	saffron gin
1²/₃oz/5cl	chamomile flowers, infused and strained
³/₄oz/2.5cl	elderflower cordial
4 sprigs	mint
3	lime wedges, juiced

GARNISH dried saffron flowers

Shake all ingredients with ice. Strain into a chilled cocktail glass. Sprinkle the saffron flowers over the drink.

Saffron Love

1²/₃oz/5cl	vodka
¹/₂oz/1.5cl	orange curaçao liqueur
¹/₂oz/1.5cl	saffron-infused syrup
¹/₂oz/1.5cl	fresh orange juice
¹/₂oz/1.5cl	honey syrup

GARNISH twist of orange

Shake all ingredients with ice. Strain into a chilled cocktail glass.

Tarra Card

1²/₃oz/5cl	saffron gin
1²/₃oz/5cl	pineapple juice
¹/₂oz/1.5cl	fresh lime juice
1 tsp	vanilla sugar
2 sprigs	fresh tarragon

GARNISH sprig of tarragon

Muddle the tarragon with the vanilla sugar and lime juice in the bottom of a shaker. Add ice and the remaining ingredients. Shake. Strain into a chilled cocktail glass. Float the garnish on top.

vanilla

Vanilla is one of the most complex flavors, with hundreds of components that create its flavor and aroma. Smooth and creamy describes most vanillas.

Barbie

1²/₃oz/5cl	gin
¹/₂oz/1.5cl	rhubarb purée
1oz/3cl	vanilla syrup
dash	gooseberry syrup

GARNISH gooseberry

Shake all ingredients with ice. Strain into a chilled cocktail glass. Add the garnish on a cocktail stick in the drink.

Kinky Martini

1²/₃oz/5cl	vanilla vodka
2¹/₂oz/4.5cl	strawberry purée
1¹/₂oz/1.5cl	strawberry liqueur
1¹/₂oz/1.5cl	coconut cream

Shake all ingredients with ice. Strain into a chilled cocktail glass.

Spongecake Martini

1³/₄oz/5cl	Matusalem rum
half	vanilla pod
half	plum
³/₄oz/2.5cl	apple juice
¹/₂oz/1.25cl	chestnut liqueur
¹/₃oz/1cl	vanilla syrup
¹/₃oz/1cl	fresh lemon juice

Muddle the vanilla pod and the plum in the bottom of a shaker. Add ice, then the remaining ingredients. Shake well. Strain into a chilled cocktail glass.

sweet & creamy

chocolate cream & honey

Sweet and creamy flavors bring a sense of well-being to the psyche. There's nothing to match rolling your tongue around your mouth to capture every last drop of pleasure.

Each of the flavors in this section—chocolate, cream, and honey—offers gorgeous rich and multilayered pleasures when combined in a cocktail with other, compatible ingredients.

To sip a glass of Baileys Original Irish Cream is to experience something unique. Made with all natural ingredients (fresh dairy cream, a triple pot still whiskey, and a natural cocoa extract from Belgium), Baileys is the world's biggest-selling liqueur.

Pure honey has a piquant sweetness of its own and is also a natural product with healthy benefits.

Chocolate has an entire range of flavors from earthy to fruity (depending on whether it is dark, milk, or white). High amounts of dairy (less cocoa bean) mean mellow, more milky and caramelized flavors. The cocoa aspect should have a hint of bitterness, but only a hint. In plain chocolate, you might discover cocoa, hints of pineapple, banana, passion fruit, vanilla, cinnamon, or even blends of these flavors. The intense aromas and perfumes of the chocolate are released evenly on the tongue before ending on a distinct final note.

Chocolate mixes well with spirits, and in particular, whiskey, bourbon, armagnac, and cognac. Rums can also provide a good spirit base for a smooth, chocolate-flavored cocktail.

In a cocktail, chocolate makes its mark strongly, with a sweet statement, but a textural layer also declares its presence.

My advice: Too much of a quality chocolate flavor can be too much of a good thing, so follow the amounts in the recipe instructions carefully.

chocolate

Depending on the type of chocolate you buy, flavors range from slightly bitter to sweet and creamy, with hints of floral, fruity, or spicy finishing notes. A good chocolate should be perfectly smooth on the tongue.

Aztec Gift

1oz/3cl	bourbon
2/3oz/2cl	dark chocolate liqueur
1/3oz/1cl	port
1/3oz/1cl	Frangelico
1/2oz/1.5cl	blueberry juice

Shake all ingredients with ice. Strain into a chilled cocktail glass.

Caribbean Mozart

1/2oz/1.5cl	rum
1 3/4oz/5cl	white chocolate liqueur
1/2oz/1.5cl	coconut syrup

GARNISH small wedge of fresh pineapple

Add ingredients to a mixing glass with ice. Stir well. Pour into a shot glass. Add the garnish on top.

Choco Kiss

1 1/3oz/4cl	mandarin vodka
1oz/3cl	dark chocolate liqueur
1 tsp	orange marmalade
2 wedges	fresh lime

GARNISH few thin strips of orange peel

Muddle the lime in the shaker. Add remaining ingredients and ice. Shake sharply. Strain into a chilled cocktail glass. Add the garnish in the drink.

Chocolate Colada

1oz/3cl	light rum
1³/₄oz/5cl	white chocolate liqueur
1oz/3cl	coconut syrup
¹/₂oz/1.5cl	heavy (double) cream
3oz/9cl	pineapple juice

Shake all ingredients with ice. Strain into a colada glass filled with ice.

Chocolate Martini

2oz/6cl	vodka
1oz/3cl	white chocolate liqueur

GARNISH dark chocolate powder

Shake the ingredients with ice. Strain into a chilled cocktail glass with a rim crusted with the dark chocolate powder.

Chocolate Rum

1oz/3cl	light rum
1 tsp	151 proof rum
1oz/3cl	white crème de cacao
¹/₂oz/1.5cl	white crème de menthe
1 Tbsp	heavy (double) cream

Shake all ingredients with ice. Strain into an old-fashioned glass filled with ice cubes. Stir.

Luxe Moment

1¹/₃oz/4cl	Pernod
1oz/3cl	white chocolate liqueur
1oz/3cl	mandarin juice
dash	honey syrup

GARNISH twist of orange

Shake all ingredients with ice. Strain into a chilled cocktail glass. Add the garnish.

cream

A good cream has the delicate sweetness of milk and a thickness that can be felt with the tongue, similar to, say, a very soft cream cheese. The flavor of cream fills the entire mouth with an enticing smoothness. There is nothing quite like its delicious flavor.

Baileys Banana Colada

2oz/6cl	**Baileys Irish Cream**
1	**banana**
1oz/3cl	**Parrot Bay rum**

GARNISH slice of banana

 Blend the ingredients with ice until smooth. Pour in a highball filled with ice. Add the garnish. Serve with a straw.

Brandy Alexander

1oz/3cl	**cognac**
1oz/3cl	**brown crème de cacao**
1oz/3cl	**heavy (double) cream**

GARNISH fresh grated nutmeg

Shake all ingredients with ice. Strain into a cocktail glass. Grate nutmeg over the drink.

Flip My Lid

1oz/3cl	**dark rum**
1/2oz/1.5cl	**port**
1/2oz/1.5cl	**Pisang Ambon liqueur**
1oz/3cl	**heavy (double) cream**
1/3oz/1cl	**honey syrup**
1	**whole pasteurized egg**

 Shake all ingredients with ice. Strain into a chilled cocktail glass. Sip slowly.

Golden Cadillac

1oz/3cl	white crème de cacao
²/₃oz/2cl	Galliano
1oz/3cl	heavy (double) cream

Shake all ingredients with ice.
Strain into a chilled cocktail glass.

Grasshopper

1oz/3cl	green crème de menthe
1oz/3cl	white crème de cacao
1oz/3cl	heavy (double) cream

Shake all ingredients with ice.
Strain into a chilled cocktail glass.

Sloe Gin Flip

1oz/3cl	sloe gin
2 Tbsps	light cream
1 barspoon	powdered sugar
1	free-range egg

GARNISH nutmeg

Shake all ingredients with ice.
Strain into an old-fashioned glass
with ice. Sprinkle nutmeg on top.

Snow Cream

2oz	Baileys Irish Cream
¹/₂ oz/1.5cl	Chambord
dash	grenadine

Shake the ingredients with ice.
Strain into a chilled cocktail glass.

honey

Honey comes in many exotic flavors these days. However, a basic pure and clear honey tastes sweet on the tongue, but not sickly sweet, and has a fine texture that blends well in cocktails.

Bee's Knees

1oz/3cl	light rum
1oz/3cl	dark rum
1oz/3cl	fresh orange juice
1/2oz/1.5cl	heavy (double) cream
1/2oz/1.5cl	milk
2 tsps	clear honey

GARNISH fresh nutmeg

Shake all ingredients with ice sharply to let everything combine well. Strain into a chilled cocktail glass. Grate the fresh nutmeg over the drink.

Chili & Honey Cocktail

1²/3oz/5cl	manuka honey vodka
half	lime
1	kaffir lime leaf
2	small slices of chili
1/2oz/1.5cl	Jägermeister
1/3oz/1cl	elderflower water
1/2oz/1.5cl	honey syrup

GARNISH kaffir lime leaves

Muddle the kaffir lime leaf with the chili in the bottom of a shaker. Add ice, then remaining ingredients. Shake. Double strain into a chilled cocktail glass. Add the garnish to the side of the glass.

Honey-tini

2oz/6cl	honey vodka
1/2oz/1.5cl	apple juice

GARNISH apple fan

Shake all ingredients with ice. Strain into a chilled cocktail glass. Add the garnish on the rim.

Honey Toddy

2oz/6cl	Scotch
1oz//3cl	clear honey
^{1}/2oz/1.5cl	fresh lemon juice
2 pieces	honeycomb
1oz/3cl	water

GARNISH twist of lemon, small piece of honeycomb

Gently warm all ingredients. Pour into a heatproof glass. Add the twist of lemon and the small honeycomb piece as a garnish.

Honey, Trust Me!

2oz/6cl	honey vodka
^{1}/2oz/1.5cl	brown crème de cacao
^{1}/2oz/1.5cl	limoncello
1oz/3cl	heavy (double) cream

GARNISH grated lemon zest

Shake all ingredients with ice. Strain into a chilled cocktail glass. Lightly grate the zest of a lemon over the top.

Honeysuckle Cocktail

1^2/3oz/5cl	light rum
^{2}/3oz/2cl	fresh lime juice
^{2}/3oz/2cl	honey syrup

Shake all ingredients with ice. Strain into a chilled cocktail glass.

Honeysuckle Daiquiri

2oz/6cl	light rum
1oz/3cl	honey syrup
1oz/3cl	fresh lemon juice
1oz/3cl	fresh orange juice

GARNISH mint leaf

Shake all ingredients with ice. Strain into a chilled cocktail glass.

unusual flavors

There are rare moments when an ingredient usually regarded as a food can be adapted for a cocktail. The skill is in selecting something to complement and enhance the food ingredient.

I was in a restaurant bar in Moscow eating smoked salmon when the owner of the restaurant asked me to create a cocktail for his bar. The flavor of the smoked salmon and its oily texture were an inspiration to me, and the resulting cocktail recipe, called Sassy Salmon, is on page 173.

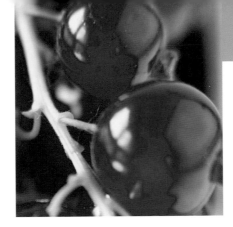

Other unusual ingredients used to flavor a cocktail include balsamic vinegar, garlic, rose petal, truffle, and the hisbiscus flower. An eclectic collection if ever there was one!

When using any of these unusual flavors, the trick is to make sure you select the freshest kind available so the full spectrum of its flavor comes through. If the item is fresh, you need only use a small bit of it. Other dried or preserved varieties are not as full of flavor as a fresh item.

True balsamic vinegar is made from the by-product at the end of the wine aging process. During the aging of an Italian artisanal balsamic the vinegar is shifted from one type of wood to the next. The cherry, chestnut, oak, and mulberry barrels all leave their imprint on the flavor of the vinegar. This brings an unbelievable concentration of sweet-sour flavor in a dense, brown-black vinegar with hints of berries, grapes, and vanilla. Balsamic vinegar goes well with fresh, sweet strawberries and sweet liqueurs.

Garlic has a sweet pungency that is released when the skin is peeled away and the garlic clove is sliced open. My advice is to not prepare the garlic in advance, but at the moment it is required.

The wild hibiscus flower is an interesting ingredient that's available in a syrup. This product gives a drink a two-fold interest. Firstly, it looks fabulous in the bottom of a champagne flute. Secondly, the syrup in which it is stored is infused with delicate floral notes.

Rose petals add a delicate flavor to champagne cocktails, and also combine well with vodka. As for the unique, woody flavor of the truffle, it can only be seen in the finest company and champagne fits that bill.

Follow the recipes exactly and you will learn about balance and the harmony of flavors that originally surprised you.

balsamic vinegar

The white and sugary Trebbiano grapes grown in the northern region of Italy near Modena provide the base of the true balsamic vinegars which are rich, sweet, and subtly woody.

Balsamic Twist

1¹/₃oz/4cl	grappa
²/₃oz/2cl	Mandarine Napoleon
¹/₃oz/1cl	maraschino liqueur
2 tsps	aged balsamic vinegar

GARNISH twist of orange

Shake all ingredients with ice.
Strain into a chilled cocktail glass.
Add the garnish.

Intrigue

1²/₃oz/5cl	cognac
1¹/₂oz/1.5cl	white crème de cacao
1¹/₂oz/1.5cl	dry white wine
²/₃oz/2cl	raspberry purée
2 tsps	balsamic vinegar
dash	honey syrup

GARNISH raspberry, mint leaves

Shake all ingredients with ice.
Strain into a chilled cocktail glass.
Add the garnish.

Maestro

1¹/₃oz/4cl	vodka
²/₃oz/2cl	crème de fraise
2 dashes	fresh lime juice
2 dashes	maple syrup
2 dashes	balsamic vinegar

GARNISH half a strawberry

Shake all ingredients with ice.
Strain into a chilled martini glass
Add the half a strawberry on the
rim of the glass.

garlic

Here's a flavor you don't expect in a cocktail. There are many garlic flavors, ranging from hot to mild and not overly pungent.

Garlic Affair

1oz/3cl	Martell VS cognac
1/2oz/1.5cl	apricot brandy
1/2oz/1.5cl	fresh lemon juice
	ginger beer
	garlic glove

GARNISH wedge of lime, maraschino cherry

Gently muddle the garlic in the bottom of a shaker. Add the remaining ingredients. Shake well. Strain into a highball filled with ice. Top up with ginger beer. Stir. Add the garnish.

hibiscus

A wild hibiscus flower has a tart and sour taste with a raspberry, rhubarb, and plum character. Because of its vibrant red color, it livens up a cocktail. You can buy them in syrup.

Hibiscus Daiquiri

2oz/6cl	light rum
1oz/3cl	fresh lime juice
1oz/3cl	wild hibiscus syrup
1	hibiscus flower from the jar

GARNISH slice of lime

Place the flower in a chilled cocktail glass, making it sit upright. Pour the remaining ingredients into a shaker with ice. Shake vigorously for 10 seconds. Strain into the glass.

rose

The petals of a rose are softly fragrant with a flavor to match. Pure rose essence is more intense than rose water, offering a beautiful floral bouquet. A spirit infused with rose petals tastes different again.

Heebie

1²/₃oz/5cl	rose vodka
²/₃oz/2cl	triple sec
1oz/3cl	pomegranate juice
dash	rose water

GARNISH pink rose petals

Shake all ingredients with ice. Strain into a chilled cocktail glass. Add the rose petals on top of the cocktail.

Rosé-tini

1²/₃oz/5cl	rose vodka
³/₄oz/2.5cl	rosé wine
¹/₂oz/1.5cl	apricot liqueur
1 barspoon	wild hibiscus flower syrup

GARNISH rose petals

Shake all ingredients with ice. Double strain into a chilled cocktail glass. Add the rose petals on top of the drink.

Spring Pink Martini

2oz/6cl	rose vodka
³/₄oz/2.5cl	rosé wine
¹/₂oz/1.5cl	Rose's lime cordial

GARNISH lime spiral

Shake all ingredients with ice. Strain into a chilled cocktail glass. Add the garnish and let it drop over the rim of the glass.

smoked salmon

The oiliness of smoked salmon is an unexpected bonus in this cocktail, blending well with vodka and lemon juice. The salmon has a salty, as well as smoked, flavor.

Sassy Salmon

1²/₃oz/5cl	vodka
1	piece smoked salmon two fingers wide
1	small piece dill
²/₃oz/2cl	dry white wine
²/₃oz/2cl	fresh lime juice
2	thin slices chili

Gently muddle the smoked salmon, dill, and chili with the lemon juice in the bottom of a shaker. Add the remaining ingredients and shake. Strain into a cocktail glass. Garnish with a piece of dill on the drink.

GARNISH sprig of dill

truffle

A truffle is prized for its unique musky flavor and aroma, regardless of whether it is a white or black truffle. Black truffles are usually used in cooking, or making martinis.

Truffle Martini

1	bottle vodka
1	whole black truffle, thinly sliced
few slices	fresh ginger
1²/₃oz/5cl	grappa
	champagne

Place the sliced truffle in the bottle. Add the ginger and grappa. With the cap on, shake the bottle. Place in the freezer for one week to infuse the flavors. *To make one cocktail:* almost fill a chilled cocktail glass with the vodka. Top up with champagne. Stir.

vegetables

Who would have thought rhubarb and grapefruit juice would go together with a measure of English gin? Or, horseradish vodka with tangerine and fresh lemon juice? In this section the recipes will open your mind as to what you can achieve with a little imagination, flair, and confidence to put a cocktail's ingredients in a shaker with each other.

The idea of vegetable juice in a nonalcoholic cocktail is not new, whereas the idea of beet juice with chilled vodka is certainly an interesting one. The fleshy, crisp and sweet capsicum (bell pepper) complements a cocktail, offering color as well as flavor, as does the aforementioned beet.

This recent predilection for cocktails with fresh vegetables is part of the trend for a healthier lifestyle without saying no to alcohol. Vodka, light rum, silver tequila, and gin are enlivened by vegetable juices in a delicious way.

Carrot, cucumber, and rhubarb are each "light" flavors and as such are good mixers in small quantities. Carrot juice is already a popular mainstream drink. When you think of mixing it, remember the flavor of carrot has an affinity with honey, raisins, cinnamon, and nutmeg as well as cream.

This is the perfect cocktail ingredient, at home with other flavors, and not dominating as a flavor.

Cucumber has an herby, sweet, and grassy flavor. Put it together with mint, vinegar, chili, lemon, and ginger and it will hold its own flavor and texture.

Rhubarb is sweet with a fabulous texture even when it has been refined through a sieve, and what a lovely color it imparts to the cocktail!

Which leaves the matter of horseradish vodka. Its hot, peppery flavor is an acquired taste, but then again, it all depends upon the other flavors used to balance its pungency.

As mentioned for all of the other flavors, always look for the freshest vegetable to obtain the freshest taste.

beet

Beets have an intense, sweet, and earthy flavor when cooked. For these recipes, small beets were roasted, and cooled then puréed until smooth.

Beet-ini

1oz/3cl	vodka
1/2oz/1.5cl	crème de fraise des bois
1oz/3cl	fresh beet purée
1oz/3cl	cranberry juice
1 tsp	vanilla sugar

GARNISH two chive "straws"

Shake all ingredients with ice. Strain into a chilled cocktail glass. Add the garnish.

Russian Experience

2oz/6cl	vodka
half	mid-sized cooked beet
dash	fresh lemon juice
	cracked black pepper
pinch	salt
1in/2.5cm	lemongrass
2	thin slices cucumber

GARNISH sprig of dill

Muddle the beet, lemon juice, and cucumber in a shaker. Add ice and the remaining ingredients. Shake. Strain into a chilled cocktail glass. Add the garnish on top of the drink.

Scarlet Mischief

1oz/3cl	apple vodka
2	roasted baby beets, diced
1/2oz/1.5cl	fresh lemon juice
1oz/3cl	lychee juice
3 barspoons	elderflower cordial
1/2oz/1.5cl	Chambord

GARNISH strawberry

Muddle the beets in the bottom of a shaker. Add ice and remaining ingredients. Shake all ingredients with ice. Double strain into a chilled cocktail glass. Add the strawberry on the rim.

lemongrass and dill decorate this beet juice and vodka drink, **Russian Experience.**

capsicum

Also known as bell pepper, this fleshy and sweet vegetable simply
bursts with juicy flavor. When eaten raw, the crisp sweetness lasts
in the mouth. Cut bell peppers into strips when muddling in the
bottom of a shaker. This action releases the flavor better.

Love to Love

1oz/3cl	vanilla rum
3	red bell pepper rings, sliced ¹⁄₄in thick
3	basil leaves
1oz/3cl	light rum
³⁄₄oz/2.5cl	fresh lime juice
¹⁄₂oz/1.5cl	fresh grapefruit juice
¹⁄₂oz/1.5cl	gomme syrup

 Gently muddle the two pepper rings and two basil leaves in a shaker. Add the remaining ingredients. Fill the shaker with ice. Shake. Strain the mixture through a fine mesh strainer into a chilled cocktail glass. Float the remaining pepper ring on top of the drink, then add the remaining basil leaf.

Rattle and Hum

1oz/3cl	silver tequila
¹⁄₂oz/1.5cl	Passoa
¹⁄₃oz/1cl	Van Der Hum
¹⁄₂oz/1.5cl	honey syrup
¹⁄₂oz/1.5cl	fresh lime juice
²⁄₃oz/2cl	guava juice
5	small pieces of yellow bell pepper

GARNISH thin strips of yellow bell pepper

 Muddle the pepper in the bottom of the shaker. Add the remaining ingredients. Shake well. Pour into an old-fashioned glass filled with crushed ice. Add the thin strips of yellow pepper. *Note: Use a blood orange when in season because this variety gives the cocktail a more intense flavor.*

Yellow bell peppers are the designated garnish for the cocktail **Rattle and Hum.**

carrot

Long, thin, and orange, the carrot contains more vitamin A than any other vegetable. A sweet and earthy flavor is dominant when carrots are freshly juiced. Look for medium-sized carrots because large ones can have a woody center and be unappetizing.

Carrot Zest

2oz/6cl	vodka
2oz/6cl	carrot juice
2oz/6cl	tomato juice
1 tsp	clear honey
1oz/3cl	fresh lemon juice
2 to 3	thin slices fresh ginger
dash	Worcestershire sauce

 Muddle the ginger in the bottom of the shaker. Add remaining ingredients and ice. Shake. Pour into a highball, letting the ice fall into the glass. Add the garnish on a cocktail stick.

GARNISH red and yellow cherry tomato, each cut in half; basil leaf

Life Saver

2oz/6cl	vodka
3oz/12cl	carrot juice
1oz/3cl	apple juice
2	thin slices ginger

 Shake all ingredients with ice. Strain into a highball filled with ice. Add the garnish on the rim.

GARNISH thin wedge of lime

Vitamin Hit

1²/3oz/5cl	vodka
2oz/6cl	carrot juice
1oz/3cl	Granny Smith apple juice
2	thin slices fresh ginger
1oz/3cl	fresh lime juice
²/3oz/2cl	elderflower liqueur

 Muddle the ginger in the shaker. Add remaining ingredients and ice. Shake. Strain into a highball filled with ice. Add the garnish.

GARNISH apple fan

cucumber

The younger, small, and slender cucumbers are usually sweeter than the larger versions. Cucumbers with waxed skins require peeling; those with seeds need the seeds removed. A good cucumber will have a fresh, succulent flavor.

C C Cooler

2oz/6cl	**Hendrick's gin**
1oz/3cl	**apple juice**
1oz/3cl	**cranberry juice**
quarter	**small cucumber, diced**
3	**mint leaves**

GARNISH slice of cucumber

Muddle the cucumber and mint in the bottom of a shaker. Add ice and remaining ingredients. Shake. Strain into a highball filled with crushed ice. Add the garnish on top of the drink. Serve with a straw.

Cool Cucumber

1½ oz/4.5cl	**Plymouth gin**
3	**slices cucumber**
1oz/3cl	**fresh orange juice**
dash	**Campari**
dash	**gomme syrup**

GARNISH slice of cucumber

Muddle the cucumber in a mixing glass. Add ice, gin, orange juice, Campari, and syrup. Shake. Strain into a chilled cocktail glass. Add the cucumber slice.

Cucumber Martini

2oz/6cl	**vodka**
quarter	**small cucumber, diced**
dash	**gomme syrup**

GARNISH cucumber spiral

Muddle the cucumber in the bottom of a shaker. Add ice and remaining ingredients. Shake. Double strain into a chilled cocktail glass. Add the garnish from the rim.

horseradish

An unusual flavor to find in a cocktail, horseradish is spicy on the tongue, with hints of pepper in the finish. The recipes here use horseradish-flavored spirits, not fresh horseradish.

Horseradish Margarita

1½oz/4.5cl	horseradish-infused tequila
½oz/1.5cl	Cointreau
¾oz/2cl	fresh lime juice
½oz/1.5cl	fresh pomegranate juice
dash	gomme syrup

GARNISH twist of lime

 Place ⅓ cup fresh horseradish, peeled and chopped, into a cup of silver tequila. Stir and let it sit for 24 hours.

Shake all ingredients with ice. Strain into an old-fashioned glass filled with ice. Add the twist of lime.

Hot Voodoo Love

1½oz/4.5cl	horseradish vodka
½oz/1.5cl	sweet vermouth
1oz/3cl	fresh lemon juice
½oz/1.5cl	tangerine juice
½oz/1.5cl	gomme syrup
dash	Angostura bitters

GARNISH orange twist

 Shake all ingredients vigorously with ice. Strain into a chilled cocktail glass. Add the garnish.

Hummer

1⅓oz/4cl	horseradish vodka
⅔oz/2cl	Cointreau
1oz/3cl	carrot juice
1⅔oz/5cl	pressed apple juice
2 dashes	ginger purée

 Shake all ingredients vigorously with ice. Strain into a chilled cocktail glass.

rhubarb

In its raw state the stalks of rhubarb are sour and unappetizing, but when stewed with sugar and strained, rhubarb juice is an exotic addition to any cocktail. Try gin, apple, and orange with it.

Rhubarb Cosmo

1¹/₃oz/4cl	vodka
²/₃oz/2cl	fresh rhubarb juice
¹/₂oz/1.5cl	triple sec or Cointreau
¹/₂oz/1.5cl	fresh lime juice

Shake all ingredients with ice.
Strain into a chilled cocktail glass.

Rhuby

1²/₃oz/5cl	cachaça
1oz/3cl	rhubarb syrup
²/₃oz/2cl	fresh lime juice

GARNISH slice of star fruit, wedge of dragon fruit

Shake all ingredients with ice.
Strain into a chilled cocktail glass.
Peel the wedge of dragon fruit and add it and the star fruit to the rim.

Spring Tao

1²/₃oz/5cl	Hendrick's gin
1oz/3cl	fresh grapefruit juice
dash	gomme syrup
4	small pieces fresh rhubarb

GARNISH rhubarb stick

Muddle the rhubarb and the syrup in the bottom of a shaker. Add the remaining ingredients. Shake well with ice. Strain through a tea strainer into an old-fashioned glass filled with ice. Add the garnish in the drink.

wine
flavors

champagne
vermouth
red & white wines

Champagne is crafted from

either Chardonnay, Pinot Noir, or Pinot
Meunier grapes, which are responsible for
its flavor. Usually of a light straw color, with
bubbles ranging in size from small to tiny,
champagne differs in flavor from house to
house and vintage to vintage. The purple
Pinot Noir grape has a colorless, sugary juice
that gives body and long life to the wine,
while the small Chardonnay grape
contributes the perfume.

Vermouth is an aromatized

wine, with its name derived from the
German word *wermut* (wormwood). This
herb was added to wine as far back as
AD 78 for medicinal purposes. Traditionally,
the Italians made sweeter, heavier
vermouths, and the French made lighter,
drier vermouths. Now both countries
produce all types of vermouth using a
combination of ingredients such as quinine,
coriander, juniper, and orange peel.

Wine is full of flavors. The

flavor of gooseberry is found in Sauvignon
wine; hints of green apple can be in a
Riesling, and a Gewürztraminer has floral
notes such as orange blossom, and spicy
flavors. A Chardonnay will fill the mouth
with luscious honeysuckle and peachy scents
with a smoky oak aroma, to name but a few
flavors. In a Cabernet you might find black
currant and raspberry flavors, while a Shiraz
might have black fruit, chocolate, and spice
delights.

champagne

A fine champagne taste is complex, with words like delicate green apple, rich, creamy, crisp, slightly tart, floral, perfume used to describe its unique flavor.

Champagne Cocktail

¹/₂oz/1.5cl	cognac
1 cube	white sugar
2 drops	Angostura aromatic bitters
	champagne

GARNISH quarter slice of orange, maraschino cherry (optional)

Take a lump of sugar with fruit tongs, holding it over a chilled champagne flute, then pour the drops of angostura over it. Place it on the bottom of the glass. Add the cognac. Top up with champagne. Pour the champagne very slowly, to prevent it bubbling over. Garnish with a quarter slice of orange.

Champagne Tropicale

1¹/₃oz/4cl	mango purée, very chilled
1oz/3cl	maraschino liqueur
	champagne

GARNISH maraschino cherry

Pour the purée into a mixing glass. Add the champagne. Stir gently to combine the two. Pour into a champagne flute and float the cherry on top.

Fifty Fizz

1¹/₃oz/4cl	raspberry purée
¹/₃oz/1cl	Bénédictine
	champagne

GARNISH two raspberries, mint leaf

Shake the purée and the Bénédictine with ice. Strain into a coupe glass. Top up with champagne. Stir carefully. Add the garnish on a toothpick.

Le Grand Cognac

1oz/3cl	cognac
6	black grapes
dash	vanilla syrup
	champagne

Muddle the grapes in the bottom of an old-fashioned glass. Add the cognac and the vanilla. Stir. Fill with crushed ice and top up with champagne. Stir gently.

Melon Fizz

quarter	canteloupe melon, diced
$^1/_2$oz/1.5cl	Cointreau
dash	gomme syrup
	champagne

GARNISH thin slice of melon

Blend all ingredients, except for champagne, with a handful of crushed ice until smooth. Double strain into a champagne coupe. Top up with champagne. Stir. Add the garnish on the rim.

Metropolis II

1oz/3cl	vodka
1oz/3cl	crème de framboise
	champagne

Shake ingredients, except champagne, with ice. Strain into a champagne coupe. Top up with champagne. Stir.

Pussycat

$^1/_2$oz/1.5cl	Parfait Amour
$^1/_2$oz/1.5cl	crème de fraise
$^2/_3$oz/2cl	raspberry purée
	champagne

GARNISH strawberry

Shake the first three ingredients with ice. Strain into a chilled champagne flute. Top up with champagne. Cut a strawberry in half, vertically, and slice a section of it to add to the side of the glass.

vermouth

The four styles of vermouth range from dry to sweet: extra dry, bianco/white, sweet/red, and rosé. French vermouths are sweet or dry, with a spicy aroma. Italian vermouths have a wider flavor base.

Alfonso XIII

1³/₄oz /4.5cl dry sherry
1³/₄oz /4.5cl red Dubonnet
slice   orange dusted with
               cinnamon

GARNISH orange peel

Muddle the orange slice and the sherry in the bottom of a shaker. Add the Dubonnet and ice. Shake. Strain into a chilled cocktail glass. Flame the orange peel.

Aviator

²/₃oz/2cl dry vermouth
²/₃oz/2cl sweet vermouth
²/₃oz/2cl red Dubonnet
²/₃oz/2cl gin

GARNISH twist of lemon

Stir all ingredients with ice in a mixing glass. Strain into a chilled cocktail glass. Add the garnish in the drink.

Italian White Sangria

1 bottle   extra dry vermouth
8oz/24cl   orange liqueur
8oz/24cl   fresh orange juice
2oz/6cl   fresh lemon juice
¹/₂ cup   superfine (caster) sugar
             sparkling mineral water
1 each   orange, lemon, lime,
               apple, thinly sliced

Combine the sugar with the liquid ingredients, except the sparkling mineral water, in a punch bowl or large pitcher until the sugar has dissolved. Chill until ready to serve. Stir in the fruit and the sparkling water. Add ice at the last moment.

Exotic flavors make the champagne cocktails **Pussycat** and **Melon Fizz** deliciously desirable.

wine

Reds have a robust, grapey flavor, and white wines have a delicate, dry flavor. A Sauvignon is dry, with grapefruit flavors, while a Semillon is sweet. Port is a fortified wine. Tawny port has a mellow nutty flavor, while ruby is fruity and spicy.

Claret Cobbler

2oz/6cl	claret (red wine)
1oz/3cl	vodka
^{1}/2oz/1.5cl	crème de framboise
slice	lemon
wedge	lime

GARNISH wedge of lime, slice of lemon

 Muddle fruit in the bottom of a shaker. Add remaining ingredients. Add ice. Shake well. Strain into a wine glass or small goblet filled with ice.

Code Red

1oz/3cl	gin
^{1}/2oz/1.5cl	limoncello
^{1}/3oz/1cl	fresh lime juice
2 tsp	gomme syrup
^{2}/3oz/2cl	red wine

 Shake all ingredients, except red wine, with ice. Strain into a chilled cocktail glass. Float the red wine over the top.

Divino

2oz/6cl	red wine
^{2}/3oz/2cl	vodka
^{2}/3oz/2cl	brown crème de cacao

 Shake all ingredients with ice. Strain into a wine glass.

Italian Surprise

3oz/9cl	Italian dry white wine
1oz/3cl	limoncello
dash	amaretto
dash	fresh lemon juice

GARNISH twist of lemon

Shake all ingredients with ice. Strain into a wine glass. Add the garnish in the drink.

Kir

¹/₂oz/1.5cl	crème de cassis
5oz/15cl	white wine

Place the crème de cassis in a wine glass. Add the white wine. Stir. If you want the drink to taste drier, reduce the amount of crème de cassis.

Port Cobbler

2¹/₂oz/7.5cl	ruby port
2 dashes	orange curaçao
half slice	orange
half slice	lemon
quarter slice	pineapple

GARNISH wedge of pineapple

Muddle the fruit in the bottom of a shaker. Add remaining ingredients. Add ice. Shake well. Strain into an old-fashioned glass filled with crushed ice. Add the garnish. Serve with a straw.

Red Eye

4oz/12cl	dry red wine
²/3oz/2cl	gomme syrup
1oz/3cl	fresh lemon juice
1oz/3cl	orange juice

GARNISH slice of orange

Shake the lemon and orange juices, and the gomme syrup with ice. Strain into a red wine glass filled with ice. Add the wine. Stir. Add the garnish on the rim of the drink.

general index

A

aperitif, 33
armagnac, 38

B

bar knife, 16
barspoon, 16, 17, 33
bartender tools, 16–17
bar terms, 33
bitter flavors, 14, 56–57
bitters, about, 56–57
blender, 16
blending drinks, 23, 33
bottle opener, 16, 17
bourbon, 50
brandy, 38–39
brut, defined, 33
build, defined, 33

C

Calvados, 39
champagne
    flavors, 185, 186
    flutes, 18
    opening/serving/storing,
        19
    saucers, 18
    stopper, 16, 17
chilling glasses, 19, 33
chopping board, 16
cocktail glasses, 18
cocktail preparation. See
    preparing cocktails

cocktail sticks, 16
coloring agents, 15
corkscrew, 16

D

dash, defined, 33
dash pourer, 16
digestif, defined, 33

E

egg white, 30

F

flavor(s) base, overview,
        36–37. See also Index by
    Ingredient
    bitters, 14, 56–57
    bourbon, 50
    brandy, 38–39
    champagne, 185, 186
    cocktail ingredients, 15
    defined, 14
    detectable tastes, 14
    drink categories by, 15
    fruits, overview, 64–65
    gin, 36, 42–43
    health-consciousness
        and, 10
    herbs, 130–131
    infusions, 11, 130–131
    nut, 144–145
    refining palate and,
        15

rum, 10, 36, 44
sake, 52
salty, 14
science of, 14–15
Scotch, 50
sharp (sour), 14
spices, 150–151
spicy, 14
sweet, 14
sweet and creamy,
    160–161
tequila, 44
trends, 8–10
unusual, 168–169
vegetable, 174–175
vodka, 10, 36, 48
whiskey, 50
wine, 185, 190
float, defined, 33
frosted/crusted rims, 24,
    33
fruits, about, 64–65. See
    also specific fruits in
    Index by Ingredient

G

garnishes, 24–29
    frosted/crusted rims
        and, 24, 33
    slices, 25
    spirals, 26–27
    tips, 25
    twists, 28–29
    wedges, 25
gin, 36, 42–43

glassware
    chilling, 19, 33
    frosted/crusted rims,
        33
    types of/selecting, 18
goblets, 18
grater, mini, 16

H
herbs, about, 130–131
highball glasses, 18
hot toddy/Irish coffee
    glasses, 18

I
ice, 30
ice bucket, 16
ice scoop, 16
infusions, 11, 130–131
ingredients, flavor and, 15

J
juicer, 16
juicing limes, 30

L
layering drinks, 22
liqueur flavors, 10

M
margarita glasses, 18
measurements, 32
mixing glasses, 16, 17, 22,
    33
modifiers, 15
muddler, 16, 17
    muddling drinks, 21, 33

N
nut flavors, about, 144–145

O
old-fashioned glasses, 18
on the rocks, 33
opening champagne, 19

P
pony jigger, 16, 17, 32
pourers, 16, 17
preparing cocktails, 20–23.
    See also garnishes
    blending drinks, 23
    frosted/crusted glass
        rims, 24, 33
    layering drinks, 22
    measurements, 32
    muddling drinks, 21, 33
    using mixing glasses, 22
    using shakers, 20
proof, defined, 33
proportions, 32

R
rum, 10, 36, 44

S
sake, 37, 52–53
salt and pepper grinders,
    16
salty flavors, 14
Scotch whiskies, 50
shake, defined, 33
shakers, 16, 17, 20
sharp (sour) flavors, 14
short drink, 33
shot glasses, 18
slices, making, 25
spices, about, 150–151
spicy flavors, 14
spiral, defined, 33
spirals, making, 26–27
spirits, storing, 19
stir, defined, 33
stirrers, 16
storing spirits and wine, 19
strawberry huller, 16
straws, 16
sweet and creamy flavors,
    160–161
sweet flavors, 14
syrups, making, 30

T
tall drink, 33
tequila, 37, 46
terms, bar, 33

tongs, 16, 17

tools, bartender, 16–17

twist, defined, 33

twists, making, 28–29

V

vegetable flavors, about,
174–175

vermouth, 185, 189

vodka

    flavors, 10, 36, 48

    for infusions, 131

    popularity, 10

W

wedges, making, 25

whiskey, 50

wine

    flavors, 185, 190

    storing, 19

wine glasses, 18

Z

zest, defined, 33

zester, 16

index by name

A

Acai Punch, 66
Acai-tini, 66
AJ II, 40
Alfonso XIII, 189
Americano, 58
Angel Face, 68
Apothecary Cocktail, 62
Apple-tini, 67
Appleton Garden, 67
Apricot Cosmo, 68
Apricot Sour, 68
Arabian Dream, 156, *157*
Aviator, 189
Aztec Gift, 162

B

B & B, 133
B B, 70
Baby Fingers, 116
Bacardi Classic Cocktail, 45
Bacardi Grapefruit
    Blossom, 87
Back in Black, 74
Bahama Todd, 45
Baileys Banana Colada,
    164
Balsamic Twist, 170
Banana Batida, 70
Banana Blaze, 70
Banana Daiquiri, 71
Barbie, 159
Basil Martini, 132
Beach Babe, 71
Bee's Knees, 166

Beet-ini, 176
Bella Donna, 92
Bella Taormina, 58
Bellini, 109
Berry Burst, 124
Big Jim Knockout Punch,
    80
Big Kiss, 154
Bitter Kiss, 87
Bitter Sweet Experiment,
    59
Blackberry Margarita, 72
Black Dog, 45
Black Door, 74
Black Russian, 82, 83
Blackthorn, 116
Blood & Sand, 78
Bloodhound, 59
Bloody Bull, 126
Bloody Mary, 127
Blueberry Caipirinha, 76
Blueberry Muffin Martini,
    76, 77
Blueberry Rocket, 76
Blue Rain, 52
Bobby Burns, 133
Body & Soul Reviver, 62
Bonito, 107
Bonnie Fizz, 72
Book Mark, 78
Brainstorm, 133
Brandy Alexander, 164
Brave Love, 116
Brazilian Berry, 75
Breakfast Martini, 104
Brother, 59

C

Caipirinha, 94
Calvados Cocktail, 40
Campari Nobile, 59
Cancun Cooler, 137
Cantaloupe Cup, 100
Cape Cod, 84
Caramello Colada, 114
Caribbean Mozart, 162
Carrot Zest, 180
Caveman Crush, 122
C C Cooler, 181
Champagne Cocktail, 186
Champagne Tropicale, 186
Champagne & Pear Drop,
    112
Charlie's Nightcap, 38
Cherry Blossom, 78
Cherry Crush, 79
Chili & Honey Cocktail,
    166
Chinese Lily, 96
Choco Kiss, 162
Chocolate Colada, 163
Chocolate Martini, 163
Chocolate Rum, 163
Cinnamon May, 154
Claret Cobbler, 190
Classic Tequila Shot, 47
Coccinella, 124
Coco Affair, 80
Cococabana, 80
Code Red, 190
Cognac Frappée, 39
Cool Cucumber, 181
Corpse Reviver 3, 62

Coutts, 122
Cucumber Martini, 181

D

Daiquiri, 94
Dark Side, 117
D'Artagnan II, 38
Deep Passion, 108
Deep Plum, 117
Deep Thinker, 134
Demon Martini, 118, 119
Demon Melon, 100
Devil's Butterfly, 84
Diamond Dog, 60
Diana's Bitter, 60
Dirty Martini, 102, 103
Divino, 190
Dolce Vita, 118

E

Effen Delicious, 72
El Cerro, 114
Elderflower Fizz, 135
Elderflower Margarita, 135
Espresso Martini, 82
Euphoria Cocktail, 132
Evening Thyme, 143

F

Fernet Cocktail, 62
Fickle Fig, 85
Fifty Casino Cocktail, 117
Fifty Fizz, 186

Fig Supreme, 85
Flip My Lid, 164
Fosbury Flip, 148
Franklin Cobbler, 124
French Passion, 108
Frenzy, 148
Frescolina, 98
Friends, 58
Frozen Mango Daiquiri, 98

G

Garibaldi, 60
Garlic Affair, 171
Gee Whizz, 88
Gibson, 42
Gillia, 58
Ginger Nut, 155
Gin Martini, 42
Godfrey, 73
Golden Cadillac, 165
Golden Dawn, 69
Golden Jubilee, 154
Grand Pepper, 156
Grasshopper, 165

H

Hazelnut-ini, 148, 149
Heebie, 172
Hibiscus Daiquiri, 171
High Heel, 75
Honeysuckle Cocktail, 167
Honeysuckle Daiquiri, 167

Honey-tini, 167
Honey Toddy, 166
Honey, Trust Me!, 167
Hong Kong, 52, 53
Horny Toad, 92
Horseradish Margarita, 182
Hot & Cold Toddy, 155
Hot Gringo, 152
Hot Voodoo Love, 182
Hummer, 182

I

Intrigue, 170
Irish Coffee, 82
Italian Surprise, 191
Italian White Sangria, 189

J

Jo Jo Sling, 112

K

Kamikaze Shooter, 94
Kentucky Derby Cooler, 138
Kinky Martini, 159
Kir, 191
Kiwi Daiquiri, 90
Kiwi Delight, 90
Kyoto Cocktail, 100

L

Last Sin, 82
Lavenderita, 136
Lavender Mojito, 136
Lavender-tini, 136
Le Grand Cognac, 187
Lemon Gin Collins, 93
Lemon Drop, 92
Lemon Meringue, 93
Level Martini, 48, *49*
Life Saver, 180
Limeade, 134
Love, Honor, and Obey, 152
Love to Love, 178
Lucy Loop, 104
Luxe Moment, 163
Lychee Crush, 96
Lychee La La, 96
Lychee Lover, 97
Lychee-tini, 97

M

Mad Mandarin, 104
Maestro, 170
Maiden's Prayer, 105
Mai Tai, 146
Mango Cosmopolitan, 99
Mango-lick, 99
Fruit Mimosa, 98
Mangorita, 99
Maiori Magic,60
Margarita, 95
Marked Man, 61, 62, 63
Mellow Yellow, 134
Melon Ball, 101

Melon Babe, 101
Melon Fizz, 187, *188*
Melon Patch, 101
Melon-tini, 101
Metropolis, 105
Metropolis II, 187
Mint Julep, 138
Mojito, 139
Monte Christo, 97
Monza, 61
Morning Margarita, 87

N

Naked Lady, 69
Naked New York, 102
Negroni, 61
New Orleans, 51
North Sea Breeze, 97

O

Old-Fashioned, 51
Orange Breeze, 105
Orange-tini, 105
Oriental Tea Party, 132

P

Papa Doble, 86
Parisian Smash, 110
Passion-tini, 109
Parisian Blossom, 110, 111
Pearadise Martini, 112
Peartini, 113
Pepper Jack, 156

Perfect Thyme, 143
Personality-ini, 102
Piña Colada, 81
Pineapple Dream, 114
Pineapple Margarita, 115
Pink Flamingo, 106
Pink Gin, 43
Pirate's Sip, 81
Pisco Sour, 95
Playboy II, 115
Pome Heights, 120
Pomegranate Julep, 120
Pomegranny, 120
Pomegrita, 120
Pome-tini, 121
Pomiri, 121
Pop a Cherry-tini, 79
Port Cobbler, 191
Possibility, 81
Pussycat, 187, *188*

R

Rama, 155
Raspberry Collins, 123
Rattle and Hum, 178, *179*
Red Eye, 191
Rhubarb Cosmo, 183
Rhuby, 183
Rogue Lemongrass, 137
Rosa Maria, 140
Rosemary Cooler, 140, *141*
Rosemary-tini, 140
Rosé-tini, 172
Rum in the Old-Fashioned
    Way, 45

Russian Experience, 176, *177*
Russian Spring Punch, 75
Rusty Nail, 51

S

Saffron Dune, 158
Saffron Love, 158
Sage Fan, 142
Sage Love, 142
Sal's St. Germain, 135
Sal's Tart, 86
Salty Dog, 86
Sangrita Shooter, 47
Sapphire Martini, 43
Sassy Salmon, 173
Sazerac, 39
Scarlet Mischief, 176
Scotch Club, 123
Screwdriver, 106
Scubarello, 139
Sensual Breeze, 81
Sexy Spring Punch, 73
Shaolin Master, 115
Sidecar, 40
Singapore Sling, 79
Slipslider, 71
Sloe Gin Fizz, 165
Smoocher, 109
Snow Cream, 165
Solero Punch, 107
Southern Sea Breeze, 69
Sparkling Sakepom, 53
Spicy Fifty, 153
Spirit Lifter, 61

Spongecake Martini, 159
Spring Pink Martini, 172
Spring Tao, 183
Spring Thyme, 143
Stealth Margarita, 153
St. James, 88–89
Strawberry Jive, 125
Strawberry Margarita, 125
Strawberry Spice, 125
Strike Out, 121
Sweet Indulgence, 85

T

Tantric Jam, 73
Tara Special, 146
Tarra Card, 158
Tawny Orange Jelly Sour, 106
Tennessee Squirrel, 146–147
Tequila Slammer, 47
Tequila Sunrise, 106
Tequil-ini, 47
Tommy's Margarita, 95
Trade Wind, 117
Tropical Butterfly, 125
Tropical Drop, 99
Truffle Martini, 173
Tuscan Pear, 113
Tutti Fruitti, 113

V

Vampiro, 127
Vanilla Melon Fizz, 128
Va-Va-Voom, *31*, 67, *147*
Velvet Touch, 88
Virgin Colada, 115
Virgin Mary, 127
Vitamin Hit, 180
Vodka Gimlet, 95
Vodka Martini, 48, 49
Vodka Sour, 93
Voodoo Breeze, 90–91

W

Wasabi Bliss, 53
Watermelon Martini, 128, 129
Watermelon Sombrero, 128
Whiskey Sour, 93
White Cosmopolitan, 84
White Sandy Beach, 71
Wisely Yours, 142
Wonderful Wild Berries, 121
Woody au Pear, 113

Y

You're So Cool, 87

Z

Zenith, 66

index by ingredient

A

acai berry (and juice), 66
 Acai Punch, 66
 Acai-tini, 66
 Zenith, 66
agave syrup
 Brother, 59
 Mangorita, 99
 Morning Margarita, 87
 Pineapple Margarita, 115
 Rosa Maria, 140
 Tommy's Margarita, 95
 Watermelon Sombrero, 128
almond, 146–147. See also amaretto
amaretto
 Italian Surprise, 191
 Tara Special, 146
 Wisely Yours, 142
amaretto liqueur, in Peartini, 113
Angostura bitters
 Baby Fingers, 116
 Bitter Kiss, 87
 Book Mark, 78
 Champagne Cocktail, 186
 Evening Thyme, 143
 Fernet Cocktail, 62
 Hong Kong, 52
 Hot Voodoo Love, 182
 Old-Fashioned, 51
 Pink Gin, 43
 Pisco Sour, 95
 Rum in the Old-Fashioned Way, 45

Rusty Nail, 51
anise, star, in Banana Blaze, 70
Aperol
 Bella Taormina, 58
 Frenzy, 148
 Friends, 58
 Gillia, 58
 Lucy Loop, 104
apple, 67
apple, fresh, in Italian White Sangria, 189
apple cider, ginger-infused, in Hot & Cold Toddy, 155
apple-flavored vodka, in Scarlet Mischief, 176
apple juice
 AJ II, 40
 Appleton Garden, 67
 Arabian Dream, 156
 Cancun Cooler, 137
 C C Cooler, 181
 Elderflower Margarita, 135
 Honey-tini, 167
 Hummer, 182
 Jo Jo Sling, 112
 Life Saver, 180
 Monza, 61
 Orange Breeze, 105
 Oriental Tea Party, 132
 Sage Fan, 142
 Spongecake Martini, 159
 Va-Va-Voom, 67
 Vitamin Hit, 180

Voodoo Breeze, 90–91
apple sour liqueur, in Apple-tini, 67
apricot, 68–69
apricot brandy, in Fosbury Flip, 148. See also brandy, apricot
apricot jam
 Apricot Cosmo, 68
 Apricot Sour, 68
apricot liqueur, in Rosé-tini, 172
apricots, dried, in Southern Sea Breeze, 69
armagnac
 Charlie's Nightcap, 38
 D'Artagnan II, 38

B

Baileys Irish Cream
 Baileys Banana Colada, 164
 Snow Cream, 165
balsamic vinegar, 169, 170
 Balsamic Twist, 170
 Intrigue, 170
 Maestro, 170
banana liqueur. See also crème de banane
Beach Babe, 71
bananas, 70–71
 Baileys Banana Colada, 164
 Banana Batida, 70
 Banana Daiquiri, 71

Beach Babe, 71

White Sandy Beach, 71

basil, fresh, 132

Basil Martini, 132

Euphoria Cocktail, 132

Love to Love, 178

Oriental Tea Party, 132

Strawberry Jive, 125

basil vodka. See vodka, basil

beef bouillon, in Bloody Bull, 126

beetroot purée, in Beet-ini, 176

beets, 176–177

Russian Experience, 176, 177

Scarlet Mischief, 176

bell pepper (capsicum), 178, 179

Love to Love, 178

Rattle and Hum, 178–179

Bénédictine, 133

B & B, 133

Bobby Burns, 133

Brainstorm, 133

Coutts, 122

Effen Delicious, 72

Fifty Fizz, 186

Singapore Sling, 79

bitter lemon. See lemon, bitter

bitters, 56–57. See also Aperol; Campari; Fernet Branca

blackberries, 72–73

Bonnie Fizz, 72

Effen Delicious, 72

Godfrey, 73

Tantric Jam, 73

Scubarello, 139

Sexy Spring Punch, 73

blackberry liqueur, in Blackberry Margarita, 72

black currant–infused aged rum, in Back in Black, 74

black currants, 74-75. See also crème de cassis

Brazilian Berry, 75

Black Door, 74

High Heel, 75

black currant tea, in Back in Black, 74

blood orange juice

Blood & Sand, 78

Rosemary Cooler, 140, 141

blueberries, 76–77

Berry Burst, 124

Blueberry Rocket, 76

Blueberry Caipirinha, 76

Blueberry Muffin Martini, 76, 77

blueberry juice, in Aztec Gift, 162

blueberry liqueur, in Blueberry Muffin Martini, 76, 77

blue curaçao liqueur

Bahama Todd, 45

Blue Rain, 52

bourbon, 50, 51

Aztec Gift, 162

Brainstorm, 133

Franklin Cobbler, 124

Hot & Cold Toddy, 155

Kentucky Derby Cooler, 138

Marked Man, 61, 62, 63

Mint Julep, 138

New Orleans, 51

Old-Fashioned, 51

Pepper Jack, 156

Southern Sea Breeze, 69

Whiskey Sour, 93

Woody au Pear, 113

Branca Menthe, in Body & Soul Reviver, 62

brandy, 38–41. See also armagnac; calvados; cognac

B & B, 133

Corpse Reviver, 3, 62

Elderflower Fizz, 135

Fernet Cocktail, 62

brandy, apricot

Angel Face, 68

Apricot Cosmo, 68

Apricot Sour, 68

Garlic Affair, 171

Golden Dawn, 69

Naked Lady, 69

Southern Sea Breeze, 69

brandy, cherry

Cherry Blossom, 78

Pop-a-Cherry-tini, 79

Singapore Sling, 79

brandy, plum
  Deep Plum, 117
  Fifty Casino Cocktail, 117
  Trade Wind, 117

C

cachaça
  Banana Batida, 70
  Blueberry Caipirinha, 76
  Brazilian Berry, 75
  Caipirinha, 94
  Mango-lick, 99
  Rhuby, 183
  Strawberry Spice, 125
calvados
  AJ II, 40
  Angel Face, 68
  Calvados Cocktail, 40
  Golden Dawn, 69
Campari
  Americano, 58
  Bitter Sweet Experiment, 59
  Bloodhound, 59
  Brother, 59
  Campari Nobile, 59
  Coccinella, 124
  Cool Cucumber, 181
  Diamond Dog, 60
  Diana's Bitter, 60
  Dolce Vita, 118
  Garibaldi, 60
  Hong Kong, 52
  Maiori Magic, 60
  Marked Man, 61, 62, 63

Monza, 61
  Negroni, 61
  Spirit Lifter, 61
  St James, 88–89
Canadian Club, in
  Manhattan, 51
cantaloupe melon
  Cantaloupe Cup, 100
  Demon Melon, 100
  Melon Babe, 101
  Melon Fizz, 187, 188, 189
cantaloupe melon juice, in
  Melon-tini, 101
caper juice, in Level
  Martini, 48, 49
caramel liqueur, in Ginger
  Nut, 155
caramel syrup, in
  Caramello Colada, 114
cardamom, in Parisian
  Blossom, 110, 111
carrot juice, 175, 180
  Carrot Zest, 180
  Hummer, 182
  Life Saver, 180
  Vitamin Hit, 180
celery salt
  Bloody Bull, 126
  Bloody Mary, 127
  Vampiro, 127
  Virgin Mary, 127
Chambord liqueur
  Raspberry Collins, 123
  Scarlet Mischief, 176
  Snow Cream, 165

chamomile flowers, in
  Saffron Dune, 158
chamomile syrup
  Champagne & Pear
    Drop, 112
  Solero Punch, 107
champagne, 185, 186–188
  Bella Donna, 92
  Bitter Kiss, 87
  Bonnie Fizz, 72
  Champagne & Pear
    Drop, 112
  Champagne Cocktail, 186
  Champagne Tropicale, 186
  Fifty Fizz, 186
  Golden Jubilee, 154
  Le Grand Cognac, 187
  Melon Fizz, 187, 188, 189
  Metropolis II, 187
  Pussycat, 187, 188, 189
  Russian Spring Punch, 75
  Sexy Spring Punch, 73
  Sparkling Sakepom, 53
  Tequila Slammer, 47
  Truffle Martini, 173
cherries, 78–79
  Book Mark, 78
  Cherry Crush, 79
  Pop a Cherry-tini, 79
cherry brandy. See brandy, cherry
  Blood & Sand, 78
  Pop-a-Cherry-tini, 79
cherry liqueur, in Playboy
  II, 115

chestnut liqueur, in
    Spongecake Martini,
    159
chili, 152–153
    Chili & Honey Cocktail,
    166
    Hot Gringo, 152
    Love, Honor, and Obey,
    152
    Sassy Salmon, 173
    Spicy Fifty, 153
    Stealth Margarita, 153
chocolate drinks, 162–163
    Aztec Gift, 162
    Caribbean Mozart, 162
    Choco Kiss, 162
    Chocolate Colada, 163
    Chocolate Martini, 163
    Chocolate Rum, 163
    Luxe Moment, 163

chocolate liqueur, in Mad
    Mandarin, 104
cilantro (coriander), 134
cinnamon, 154
    Alfonso XIII, 189
    Banana Blaze, 70
    Strawberry Spice, 125
cinnamon syrup
    Book Mark, 78
    Cinnamon May, 154
citrus-flavored vodka, in
    Spring Thyme, 143
claret. See wine, red
cloves, in Banana Blaze, 70
club soda
    Americano, 58
    Back in Black, 74
    Bitter Sweet Experiment,
    59
    Lemon Gin Collins, 93

Melon Patch, 101
Mint Julep, 138
Negroni, 61
Old-Fashioned, 51
Raspberry Collins, 123
Scubarello, 139
Wonderful Wild Berries,
    121
You're So Cool, 87
coconut, 80–81
    about, 80
    Vanilla Melon Fizz, 128
coconut cream
    Big Jim Knockout
    Punch, 80
    Caramello Colada, 114
    Cococabana, 80
    Coco Affair, 80
    Kinky Martini, 159
    Pirate's Sip, 81

Possibility, 81
Piña Colada, 81
Tropical Drop, 99
Virgin Colada, 115
White Sandy Beach, 71
coconut rum. *See* rum,
   coconut
coconut syrup
   Cancun Cooler, 137
   Caribbean Mozart, 162
   Chocolate Colada, 163
coffee, 82–83
   Black Russian, 82, 83
   Espresso Martini, 82
   Irish Coffee, 82
   Last Sin, 82
cognac
   Banana Blaze, 70
   Body & Soul Reviver, 62
   Brandy Alexander, 164
   Champagne & Pear
     Drop, 112
   Champagne Cocktail, 186
   Cherry Blossom, 78
   Cognac Frappée, 39
   French Passion, 108
   Garlic Affair, 171
   Godfrey, 73
   Intrigue, 170
   Le Grand Cognac, 187
   Parisian Smash, 110
   Sazerac, 39
   Shaolin Master, 115
   Sidecar, 40
Cointreau
   Apple-tini, 67

Breakfast Martini, 104
Calvados Cocktail, 40
Devil's Butterfly, 84
Fifty Casino Cocktail, 117
Frescolina, 98
Horny Toad, 92
Horseradish Margarita,
   182
Hummer, 182
Kamikaze Shooter, 94
Maiden's Prayer, 105
Margarita, 95
Melon Fizz, 187, 188, 189
Morning Margarita, 87
Orange-tini, 105
Rhubarb Cosmo, 183
Rosa Maria, 140
Sidecar, 40
Singapore Sling, 79
Spirit Lifter, 61
Strike Out, 121
Watermelon Sombrero,
   128
White Cosmopolitan, 84
condensed consommé, in
   Bloody Bull, 126
coriander
   Deep Thinker, 134
   Limeade, 134
   Mellow Yellow, 134
   Rogue Lemongrass, 137
cranberry flavor, 84
cranberry juice
   Apricot Cosmo, 68
   Beet-ini, 176
   Cape Cod, 84

C C Cooler, 181
   Devil's Butterfly, 84
   Mango Cosmopolitan, 99
   Monte Christo, 97
   Orange Breeze, 105
   Oriental Tea Party, 132
   Pink Flamingo, 106
   Rama, 155
   Sensual Breeze, 81
cranberry juice, white, in
   White Cosmopolitan, 84
cream, 164–165
cream, heavy (double)
   B B, 70
   Bee's Knees, 166
   Brandy Alexander, 164
   Chocolate Colada, 163
   Chocolate Rum, 163
   Coco Affair, 80
   Flip My Lid, 164
   Golden Cadillac, 165
   Grasshopper, 165
   Honey, Trust Me!, 167
   Mad Mandarin, 104
   Virgin Colada, 115
   White Sandy Beach, 71
cream, light, in Sloe Gin
   Fizz, 165
cream, whipped, in Irish
   Coffee, 82
crème de banane liqueur
   Banana Blaze, 70
   B B, 70
   Slipslider, 71
crème de cacao, brown
   Brandy Alexander, 164

Divino, 190
Honey, Trust Me!, 167
crème de cacao, in
  Blueberry Muffin
  Martini, 76, 77
crème de cacao, white,
  B B, 70
  Chocolate Rum, 163
  Golden Cadillac, 165
  Grasshopper, 165
  Hazelnut-ini, 148, 149
  Intrigue, 170
  Wisely Yours, 142
crème de cassis
  Back in Black, 74
  Berry Burst, 124
  Brazilian Berry, 75
  Black Door, 74
  High Heel, 75
  Kir, 191
  Russian Spring Punch, 75
crème de fraise
  Franklin Cobbler, 124
  Maestro, 170
  Pussycat, 187, 188, 189
crème de framboise
  Claret Cobbler, 190
  Metropolis II, 187
  Pop a Cherry-tini, 79
crème de menthe, green,
  in Grasshopper, 165
crème de menthe, white
  Apothecary Cocktail, 62
  Chocolate Rum, 163
  Corpse Reviver 3, 62
crème de mûre
  Bonnie Fizz, 72

Effen Delicious, 72
Godfrey, 73
Scubarello, 139
Sexy Spring Punch, 73
crème de noisette. *See*
  hazelnut liqueur
  (crème de noisette)
crème de Noyaux, in
  Tennessee Squirrel,
  146–147
crème de peche, in
  Lavenderita, 136
cucumber, 181
  C C Cooler, 181
  Cool Cucumber, 181
  Cucumber Martini, 181
  Russian Experience, 176,
  177
currant-flavored vodka, in
  Black Door, 74

D

dark chocolate liqueur
  Aztec Gift, 162
  Choco Kiss, 162
dark rum. *See* rum, dark
dill, in Sassy Salmon, 173
Drambuie
  Lemon Meringue, 93
  Rusty Nail, 51
dry vermouth. *See*
  vermouth, dry

E

egg
  Flip My Lid, 164
  Sloe Gin Fizz, 165
egg white
  Apricot Sour, 68
  Bitter Sweet Experiment,
  59
  Brave Love, 116
  Sal's St. Germain, 135
  Scotch Club, 123
  Vodka Sour, 93
  Whiskey Sour, 93
egg white powder, in Pisco
  Sour, 95
egg yolk, in Fosbury Flip,
  148
elderflower, 135
elderflower cordial
  Bitter Sweet Experiment,
  59
  Chili & Honey Cocktail,
  166
  Deep Thinker, 134
  Elderflower Fizz, 135
  Elderflower Margarita,
  135
  Saffron Dune, 158
  Scarlet Mischief, 176
  Spicy Fifty, 153
  Stealth Margarita, 153
  Tropical Butterfly, 125
elderflower liqueur
  Sal's St Germain, 135
  Vitamin Hit, 180
espresso coffee

Espresso Martini, 82

Last Sin, 82

F

Fernet Branca

Apothecary Cocktail, 62

Body & Soul Reviver, 62

Corpse Reviver 3, 62

Fernet Cocktail, 62

figs, 85

Fickle Fig, 85

Fig Supreme, 85

Southern Sea Breeze, 69

Sweet Indulgence, 85

fraise de bois, in Beet-ini,
176

framboise, in Scubarello,
139

Frangelico. See also hazelnut liqueur

Aztec Gift, 162

Fosbury Flip, 148

Frenzy, 148

Hazelnut-ini, 148, 149

Last Sin, 82

Slipslider, 71

fruits, 64–65. See also
specific fruits

G

Galliano liqueur

El Cerro, 114

Golden Cadillac, 165

Vanilla Melon Fizz, 128

garlic, in Garlic Affair, 169,
171

gin, 36, 42–43. See also
Hendrick's Gin

Angel Face, 68

Aviator, 189

Baby Fingers, 116

Barbie, 159

Bella Taormina, 58

Bittersweet Experiment,
59

Bonnie Fizz, 72

Breakfast Martini, 104

Cherry Crush, 79

Coccinella, 124

Code Red, 190

Demon Martini, 118,
119

Fifty Casino Cocktail,
117

Friends, 58

Gibson, 42

Ginger Nut, 155

Gin Martini, 42

Golden Dawn, 69

Golden Jubilee, 154

Jo Jo Sling, 112

Kyoto Cocktail, 100

Lemon Gin Collins, 93

Lucy Loop, 104

Lychee La La, 96

Maiden's Prayer, 105

Mellow Yellow, 134

Negroni, 61

North Sea Breeze, 97

Orange-tini, 105

Tantric Jam, 73

Pearadise Martini, 112

Perfect Thyme, 143

Pink Gin, 43

Pomegranny, 120

Pomegrita, 120

Sapphire Martini, 43

Singapore Sling, 79

Strawberry Jive, 125

Tropical Butterfly, 125

gin, Plymouth

Caveman Crush, 122

Cool Cucumber, 181

Diana's Bitter, 60

gin, saffron

Saffron Dune, 158

Tarra Card, 158

ginger ale, in Cancun
Cooler, 137

ginger beer

Caveman Crush, 122

Garlic Affair, 171

Ginger Nut, 155

ginger cordial, in French
Passion, 108

ginger-infused apple cider,
in Hot & Cold Toddy,
155

ginger liqueur, in Tuscan
Pear, 113

ginger purée, in Hummer,
182

ginger, 155

Carrot Zest, 180

French Passion, 108

Ginger Nut, 155

Hot & Cold Toddy, 155
Life Saver, 180
Marked Man, 61, 62, 63
Perfect Thyme, 143
Truffle Martini, 173
Vitamin Hit, 180
golden mango liqueur, in
    Tropical Drop, 99
Goldschläger
    Big Kiss, 154
    Golden Jubilee, 154
gomme syrup
    AJ II, 40
    Basil Martini, 132
    Bonnie Fizz, 72
    Cantaloupe Cup, 100
    Code Red, 190
    Cucumber Martini, 181
    Daiquiri, 94
    Demon Melon, 100
    Diana's Bitter, 60
    Fernet Cocktail, 62
    Franklin Cobbler, 124
    Hot Voodoo Love, 182
    Kiwi Delight, 90
    Last Sin, 82
    Lavender-tini, 136
    Lemon Gin Collins, 93
    Lemon Drop, 92
    Lemon Meringue, 93
    Lychee Crush, 96
    Lychee La La, 96
    Melon Babe, 101
    Melon Fizz, 187, 188, 189
    Metropolis, 105
    Monza, 61

Papa Doble, 86
Peartini, 113
Pepper Jack, 156
Pisco Sour, 95
Pome Heights, 120
Pome-tini, 121
Pomiri, 121
Raspberry Collins, 123
Red Eye, 191
Rogue Lemongrass, 137
Russian Spring Punch, 75
Southern Sea Breeze, 69
Spring Tao, 183
St. James, 88–89
Strawberry Jive, 125
Tommy's Margarita, 95
Trade Wind, 117
Tuscan Pear, 113
Vanilla Melon Fizz, 128
Vodka Sour, 93
Wasabi Bliss, 53
Watermelon Martini,
    128, 129
Whiskey Sour, 93
gomme syrup infused with
    ginger, in Rama, 155
gooseberry syrup, in
    Barbie, 159
Grand Marnier
    Bonito, 107
    Dark Side, 117
    D'Artagnan II, 38
    Deep Passion, 108
    Fig Supreme, 85
    Godfrey, 73
    Grand Pepper, 156

Mangorita, 99
Velvet Touch, 88
Stealth Margarita, 153
grapefruit, 86–87
grapefruit juice
    Bacardi Grapefruit
        Blossom, 87
    Bitter Kiss, 87
    Bloodhound, 59
    Brother, 59
    Dolce Vita, 118
    Love to Love, 178
    Lychee Lover, 97
    Morning Margarita, 87
    North Sea Breeze, 97
    Papa Doble, 86
    Rogue Lemongrass, 137
    Sal's Tart, 86
    Salty Dog, 86
    Spring Tao, 183
    You're So Cool, 87
grapes
    Jo Jo Sling, 112
    Le Grand Cognac, 187
grappa
    Balsamic Twist, 170
    Fickle Fig, 85
    Truffle Martini, 173
green apple purée, in
    Spring Thyme, 143
green tea liqueur, in
    Zenith, 66
grenadine
    Arabian Dream, 156
    Bacardi Classic Cocktail,
        45

Big Jim Knockout Punch, 80

El Cerro, 114

Fickle Fig, 85

Fig Supreme, 85

Fosbury Flip, 148

Golden Dawn, 69

Naked Lady, 69

Rosemary Cooler, 140, *141*

Snow Cream, 165

Sparkling Sakepom, 53

Tequila Sunrise, 106

You're So Cool, 87

guava, 88–89

Gee Whizz, 88

Rattle and Hum, 178–179

St. James, 88–89

Velvet Touch, 88

H

Havana Club 7-year rum, in Last Sin, 82

hazelnut, 148–149

hazelnut liqueur (crème de noisette). *See also* Frangelico

Big Kiss, 154

Frenzy, 148

Ginger Nut, 155

Hendrick's gin

C C Cooler, 181

Spring Tao, 183

Tawny Orange Jelly Sour, 106

herbs, 130–143. *See also specific herbs*

hibiscus flower, Hibiscus in Daiquiri, 169, 171

honey, 166–167

honey, clear

B B, 70

Bee's Knees, 166

Bittersweet Experiment, 59

Carrot Zest, 180

Caveman Crush, 122

Chili & Honey Cocktail, 166

Coutts, 122

Fickle Fig, 85

Honey Toddy, 166

Sal's Tart, 86

Sweet Indulgence, 85

Velvet Touch, 88

honeycomb, in Honey Toddy, 166

honeydew melon juice, in Melon-tini, 101

honey syrup

Flip My Lid, 164

Honeysuckle Cocktail, 167

Honeysuckle Daiquiri, 167

Intrigue, 170

Luxe Moment, 163

Pomegranate Julep, 120

Rattle and Hum, 178–179

Saffron Love, 158

Sage Fan, 142

Spicy Fifty, 153

Tawny Orange Jelly Sour, 106

honey vodka. *See* vodka, honey

horseradish-infused tequila, in Horseradish Margarita, 182

horseradish vodka. *See* vodka, horseradish

I

Irish cream liqueur, in Slipslider, 71

Irish whiskey, in Irish Coffee, 82

J

Jack Daniels, in Tennessee Squirrel, 146–147

Jägermeister, in Chili & Honey Cocktail, 166

K

kaffir lime leaf, in Chili & Honey Cocktail, 166

Kahlua

Black Russian, 82, 83

Espresso Martini, 82

kiwi fruit, 90

Kiwi Daiquiri, 90

Kiwi Delight, 90

Lychee Crush, 96

Pepper Jack, 156

Tantric Jam, 73

Voodoo Breeze, 90–91

kiwi liqueur, in Cinnamon May, 154

kumquats

Cinnamon May, 154

Wisely Yours, 142

L

lavender, 136

Lavenderita, 136

Lavender Mojito, 136

lavender-flavored vodka, in Lavender-tini, 136

lemon, 92–93

Acai Punch, 66

Claret Cobbler, 190

Italian White Sangria, 189

Kentucky Derby Cooler, 138

Kyoto Cocktail, 100

Lychee La La, 96

Port Cobbler, 191

lemon, bitter

Campari Nobile, 59

Pomegranny, 120

lemongrass, 137

Cancun Cooler, 137

Love, Honor, and Obey, 152

Lychee La La, 96

Perfect Thyme, 143

Rogue Lemongrass, 137

Russian Experience, 176, *177*

Zenith, 66

lemongrass cordial, in Hot Gringo, 152

lemon juice

Apricot Sour, 68

Bella Donna, 92

Bloody Bull, 126

Bloody Mary, 127

Blue Rain, 52

Bonnie Fizz, 72

Breakfast Martini, 104

Cancun Cooler, 137

Caramello Colada, 114

Carrot Zest, 180

Caveman Crush, 122

Cherry Blossom, 78

Cherry Crush, 79

Chinese Lily, 96

Deep Plum, 117

Euphoria Cocktail, 132

Frenzy, 148

Garlic Affair, 171

Godfrey, 73

High Heel, 75

Honeysuckle Daiquiri, 167

Honey Toddy, 166

Horny Toad, 92

Hot Voodoo Love, 182

Italian Surprise, 191

Italian White Sangria, 189

Jo Jo Sling, 112

Kiwi Delight, 90

Lavender-tini, 136

Lemon Gin Collins, 93

Lemon Drop, 92

Lemon Meringue, 93

Brave Love, 116

Lucy Loop, 104

Lychee Crush, 96

Lychee Lover, 97

Maiden's Prayer, 105

Mango Cosmopolitan, 99

Maiori Magic, 60

Mellow Yellow, 134

Melon Babe, 101

Metropolis, 105

Morning Margarita, 87

Naked Lady, 69

Parisian Blossom, 110, *111*

Pearadise Martini, 112

Tutti Fruitti, 113

Peartini, 113

Raspberry Collins, 123

Red Eye, 191

Russian Experience, 176, *177*

Russian Spring Punch, 75

Sage Fan, 142

Sal's St. Germain, 135

Scarlet Mischief, 176

Scotch Club, 123

Sexy Spring Punch, 73

Shaolin Master, 115

Sidecar, 40

Singapore Sling, 79

Southern Sea Breeze, 69

Spongecake Martini, 159

Stealth Margarita, 153

Strawberry Jive, 125

Tawny Orange Jelly
Sour, 106

Tennessee Squirrel,
146, *147*

Vampiro, 127

Vanilla Melon Fizz, 128

Virgin Mary, 127

Vodka Sour, 93

Whiskey Sour, 93

Zenith, 66

lemon sorbet, in Mellow
Yellow, 134

lemon vodka. *See* vodka,
lemon

Licor 43, in Limeade, 134

licorice-infused cachaca, in
Mango-lick, 99

Lillet Rouge, in Evening
Thyme, 143

lime, 94–95

Acai Punch, 66

Blueberry Caipirinha, 76

Caipirinha, 94

Choco Kiss, 162

Chili & Honey Cocktail,
166

Claret Cobbler, 190

Deep Thinker, 134

French Passion, 108

Italian White Sangria,
189

Mango-lick, 99

Monte Christo, 97

Pepper Jack, 156

Saffron Dune, 158

Spring Thyme, 143

lime juice

Appleton Garden, 67

Apricot Cosmo, 68

Bacardi Classic Cocktail,
45

Banana Batida, 70

Banana Daiquiri, 71

Bitter Sweet Experiment,
59

Blackberry Margarita, 72

Blueberry Muffin
Martini, 76, *77*

Bonito, 107

Brother, 59

Cantaloupe Cup, 100

Code Red, 190

Coutts, 122

Black Door, 74

Daiquiri, 94

Dark Side, 117

Deep Passion, 108

Demon Melon, 100

Diana's Bitter, 60

Dolce Vita, 118

Elderflower Margarita,
135

Fig Supreme, 85

Fosbury Flip, 148

Frescolina, 98

Frozen Mango Daiquiri,
98

Fruit Mimosa, 98

Gee Whizz, 88

Hibiscus Daiquiri, 171

Honeysuckle Cocktail,
167

Horseradish Margarita,
182

Hot Gringo, 152

Kamikaze Shooter, 94

Kiwi Daiquiri, 90

Lavender Mojito, 136

Limeade, 134

Love, Honor, and Obey,
152

Love to Love, 178

Maestro, 170

Mai Tai, 146

Mangorita, 99

Margarita, 95

Mojito, 139

Oriental Tea Party, 132

Papa Doble, 86

Pineapple Dream, 114

Pink Flamingo, 106

Pirate's Sip, 81

Pisco Sour, 95

Playboy II, 115

Pome-tini, 121

Pomiri, 121

Pop a Cherry tini, 79

Rattle and Hum, 178, *179*

Rhubarb Cosmo, 183

Rhuby, 183

Rosa Maria, 140

Rosemary Cooler, 140,
141

Sage Love, 142

Sal's Tart, 86

Sangrita Shooter, 47

Sassy Salmon, 173
Scubarello, 139
Solero Punch, 107
Spicy Fifty, 153
St. James, 88–89
Strawberry Margarita, 125
Strike Out, 121
Sweet Indulgence, 85
Tarra Card, 158
Tommy's Margarita, 95
Trade Wind, 117
Va-Va-Voom, 67
Velvet Touch, 88
Vitamin Hit, 180
Voodoo Breeze, 90–91
Wasabi Bliss, 53
Watermelon Sombrero, 128
White Cosmopolitan, 84
Wonderful Wild Berries, 121
limoncello
Bella Donna, 92
Bella Taormina, 58
Campari Nobile, 59
Code Red, 190
Frenzy, 148
Honey, Trust Me!, 167
Italian Surprise, 191
Lemon Gin Collins, 93
Maori Magic, 60
Marked Man, 61, 62, 63
Mellow Yellow, 134
Sage Fan, 142
Spring Thyme, 143
Tuscan Pear, 113

lychee fruit, 96–97
about, 96
Lychee La La, 96
lychee juice/syrup
Lychee-tini, 97
Monte Christo, 97
North Sea Breeze, 97
Scarlet Mischief, 176
lychee liqueur
Chinese Lily, 96
Lychee Crush, 96
Lychee Lover, 97
Lychee-tini, 97
lychee purée, in Chinese Lily, 96

M

Maker's Mark bourbon, in Marked Man, 61, 62, 63
Mandarine Napoleon
Balsamic Twist, 170
French Passion, 108
Metropolis, 105
mandarin juice, in Luxe Moment, 163
mandarin liqueur
Bella Taormina, 58
Lucy Loop, 104
Mad Mandarin, 104
Rama, 155
Sage Love, 142
Solero Punch, 107
mandarin vodka. See vodka, mandarin
mango, 98–99

Frozen Mango Daiquiri, 98
Fruit Mimosa, 98
Mango-lick, 99
mango-infused cachaça, in Mango-lick, 99
mango liqueur
Frozen Mango Daiquiri, 98
Mango-lick, 99
Tropical Drop, 99
mango purée
Champagne Tropicale, 186
Frescolina, 98
Mangorita, 99
mango rum, in Mango Cosmopolitan, 99
mango syrup, in Rosemary Cooler, 140, 141
manuka honey vodka, in Chili & Honey Cocktail, 166
maple syrup
Kentucky Derby Cooler, 138
Maestro, 170
maraschino liqueur
Bacardi Grapefruit Blossom, 87
Balsamic Twist, 170
Champagne Tropicale, 186
Cherry Crush, 79
Deep Plum, 117
Papa Doble, 86

Pomiri, 121

Martell cognac, in Garlic
   Affair, 171

Matusalem rum, in
   Spongecake Martini,
159

melon
   Canteloupe Cup, 100
   Demon Melon, 100

melon drinks, 100–101
   Cantaloupe Cup, 100
   Demon Melon, 100
   Kyoto Cocktail, 100
   Melon Babe, 101
   Melon Ball, 101
   Melon Patch, 101
   Melon-tini, 101

melon liqueur
   Cococabana, 80
   Kyoto Cocktail, 100
   Melon Ball, 101
   Melon Patch, 101
   Voodoo Breeze, 90–91

milk, in Bee's Knees, 166

mineral water. *See also*
   sparkling water
   Big Kiss, 154
   Kiwi Delight, 90
   Melon Babe, 101

mint, fresh, 138–139
   Acai Punch, 66
   C C Cooler, 181
   Franklin Cobbler, 124
   Kentucky Derby Cooler,
   138
   Lavender Mojito, 136

Marked Man, 61, 62, 63
Mint Julep, 138
Mojito, 139
Parisian Smash, 110
Pomegranate Julep, 120
Saffron Dune, 158
Strawberry Jive, 125
Va-Va-Voom, 67

N

nonalcoholic drinks
   Kiwi Delight, 90
   Virgin Colada, 115
   Virgin Mary, 127
   White Sandy Beach, 71

nut flavors, 144–149

nutmeg, in Solero Punch,
   107

nutmeg syrup, in Shaolin
   Master, 115

O

olives, 102
   Dirty Martini, 102, 103
   Naked New York, 102
   Personality-ini, 102

orange bitters
   Banana Blaze, 70
   Beach Babe, 71
   Body & Soul Reviver, 62
   Fifty Casino Cocktail, 117
   Garibaldi, 60
   Mad Mandarin, 104
   Orange-tini, 105

Rogue Lemongrass, 137
Sal's St. Germain, 135
Tantric Jam, 73

orange curaçao
   Cherry Blossom, 78
   El Cerro, 114
   Mai Tai, 146
   Port Cobbler, 191
   Saffron Love, 158

orange juice
   Acai Punch, 66
   Beach Babe, 71
   Bee's Knees, 166
   Bella Taormina, 58
   Big Jim Knockout
     Punch, 80
   Bonito, 107
   Calvados Cocktail, 40
   Campari Nobile, 59
   Cantaloupe Cup, 100
   Coco Affair, 80
   Cool Cucumber, 181
   D'Artagnan II, 38
   Diamond Dog, 60
   Deep Plum, 117
   Fosbury Flip, 148
   Fruit Mimosa, 98
   Ginger Nut, 155
   Golden Dawn, 69
   Honeysuckle Daiquiri,
     167
   Italian White Sangria,
     189
   Lucy Loop, 104
   Mad Mandarin, 104
   Maiden's Prayer, 105

Marked Man, 61, 62, 63

Orange Breeze, 105

Red Eye, 191

Rosemary Cooler, 140, *141*

Saffron Love, 158

Sal's St Germain, 135

Screwdriver, 106

Singapore Sling, 79

Spirit Lifter, 61

Tara Special, 146

Tequila Sunrise, 106

Tuscan Pear, 113

Wisely Yours, 142

orange liqueur, in Italian White Sangria, 189

orange marmalade

Breakfast Martini, 104

Choco Kiss, 162

Morning Margarita, 87

oranges, fresh, 104

Acai Punch, 66

Alfonso XIII, 189

Franklin Cobbler, 124

Italian White Sangria, 189

Parisian Smash, 110

Port Cobbler, 191

Solero Punch, 107

oregano, 139

Pop a Cherry-tini, 79

Scubarello, 139

orgeat syrup

Chinese Lily, 96

Mai Tai, 146

ouzo, in Strike Out, 121

P

Parfait Amour

Euphoria Cocktail, 132

Lavenderita, 136

Pussycat, 187, 188, 189

Sapphire Martini, 43

Parrot Bay rum, in Baileys Banana Colada, 164

passion fruit, 107–109

Deep Passion, 108

Effen Delicious, 72

French Passion, 108

Monza, 61

Pop a Cherry-tini, 79

Smoocher, 109

Tennessee Squirrel, 146–147

You're So Cool, 87

passion fruit juice

Bonito, 107

Deep Passion, 108

Dolce Vita, 118

Tropical Butterfly, 125

Sage Love, 142

passion fruit purée

French Passion, 108

Passion-tini, 109

passion fruit syrup

Tennessee Squirrel, 146, *147*

Va-Va-Voom, 67

passion fruit vodka in Pop-a-Cherry-tini, 79

Passoa liqueur

Champagne & Pear Drop, 112

Rattle and Hum, 178–179

peach, 109–111

peach and passion fruit syrup, in Smoocher, 109

peaches, fresh, in Parisian Smash, 110

peach liqueur

Parisian Smash, 110

Tantric Jam, 73

peach purée

Bellini, 109

Parisian Blossom, 110, *111*

Tara Special, 146

pear, 112–113

pear-flavored vodka. *See* vodka, pear flavored

pear juice, in Jo Jo Sling, 112

pear liqueur

Blue Rain, 52

Charlie's Nightcap, 38

Pearadise Martini, 112

pear purée

Champagne & Pear Drop, 112

Pearadise Martini, 112

Tutti Frutti, 113

Tropical Butterfly, 125

Woody au Pear, 113

pears, fresh, in Jo Jo Sling, 112

Peche de Vigne, in Parisian Blossom, 110, *111*

pepper, bell. *See* bell pepper (capsicum)

pepper, black, 156–157
    Arabian Dream, 156
    Bloody Mary, 127
    Russian Experience, 176,
        177
    Sangrita Shooter, 47
    Vampiro, 127
    Virgin Mary, 127
peppercorns, pink, in
    Grand Pepper, 156
pepper vodka, in Pepper
    Jack, 156
Pernod
    Luxe Moment, 163
    Rosemary-tini, 140
    Strike Out, 121
Peychaud bitters
    New Orleans, 51
    Sazerac, 39
pineapple, 114–115
pineapple, fresh
    Pineapple Dream, 114
    Pineapple Margarita, 115
    Port Cobbler, 191
pineapple juice
    Bahama Todd, 45
    Cancun Cooler, 137
    Caramello Colada, 114
    Chocolate Colada, 163
    Cococabana, 80
    Coco Affair, 80
    El Cerro, 114
    Gee Whizz, 88
    Sensual Breeze, 81
    Melon Ball, 101
    Pina Colada, 81, 114

Pineapple Dream, 114
Pineapple Margarita, 115
Playboy II, 115
Pome Heights, 120
Sage Love, 142
Shaolin Master, 115
Singapore Sling, 79
Tarra Card, 158
Tropical Drop, 99
Virgin Colada, 115
White Sandy Beach, 71
pineapple rum. See rum,
    pineapple-flavored
Pisang liqueur, in Flip My
    Lid, 164
pisco, in Pisco Sour, 95
plum brandy. See brandy,
    plum
plums, 116, 117
    Dark Side, 117
    Spongecake Martini, 159
Plymouth gin. See gin,
    Plymouth
Poire William liqueur, in
    Woody au Pear, 113
pomegranate, 118–121
    Demon Martini, 118, 119
    Pomegrita, 120
pomegranate juice
    Dolce Vita, 118
    Heebie, 172
    Horseradish Margarita,
        182
    Pome Heights, 120
    Pomegranate Julep, 120
    Pomegranny, 120

Pome-tini, 121
Pomiri, 121
Sparkling Sakepom, 53
Strike Out, 121
Wonderful Wild Berries,
    121
port
    Aztec Gift, 162
    Back in Black, 74
    Flip My Lid, 164
port, ruby, in Port Cobbler,
    191
port, vintage, in Book
    Mark, 78
prosecco (Italian sparkling
    wine)
    Bellini, 110
    Fickle Fig, 85
    Fruit Mimosa, 98
    Tara Special, 146
    Tutti Fruitti, 113
Punt e Mes, in Apothecary
    Cocktail, 62

R
raspberries, 122–123
    Brazilian Berry, 75
    Caveman Crush, 122
    High Heel, 75
    Raspberry Collins, 123
    Scotch Club, 123
    Scubarello, 139
    Tara Special, 146
raspberry juice, in Brave
    Love, 116

raspberry liqueur
Caveman Crush, 122
Monte Christo, 97
Scotch Club, 123
raspberry purée
Campari Nobile, 59
Coutts, 122
Fifty Fizz, 186
Intrigue, 170
Pussycat, 187, 188, 189
You're So Cool, 87
raspberry vodka, in
Raspberry Collins,
123
red Dubonnet
Alfonso XIII, 189
Aviator, 189
red wine. See wine, red

reposado tequila, in
Indulgence, 85
rhubarb, in Spring Tao, 183
rhubarb juice, in Rhubarb
Cosmo, 183
rhubarb purée, in Barbie,
159
rhubarb syrup, in Rhuby,
183
rose, 169, 172
rosé
Rosé-tini, 172
Spring Pink Martini, 172
rosemary, 140–141
Rosa Maria, 140
Rosemary Cooler, 140, 141
rosemary-infused vodka, in
Rosemary-tini, 140

Rose's lime cordial
Diamond Dog, 60
Spring Pink Martini,
172
Vodka Gimlet, 95
rose syrup
Bella Donna, 92
Devil's Butterfly, 84
rose vodka. See vodka, rose
rose water, in Heebie, 172
ruby port, in Port Cobbler,
191
rum, 10, 36, 44–45
Appleton Garden, 67
Caribbean Mozart, 162
Papa Doble, 86
rum, aged
Fosbury Flip, 148

Mai Tai, 146
Playboy II, 115
Rum in the Old-
Fashioned Way, 45
St. James, 88, *89*
rum, Bacardi, in Bacardi
Grapefruit Blossom, 87
rum, Bacardi white, in
Piña Colada, 81
rum, black currant-infused
añejo, in Back in Black,
74
rum, Charbay, in Lavender
Mojito, 136
rum, coconut
Bahama Todd, 45
Big Jim Knockout
Punch, 80
Cococabana, 80
Coco Loco, 81
Malibu Bay Breeze, 81
Tropical Drop, 99
rum, dark
Bahama Todd, 45
Bee's Knees, 166
Big Jim Knockout
Punch, 80
Coco Loco, 81
El Cerro, 114
Flip My Lid, 164
Pome Heights, 120
Shaolin Master, 115
Solero Punch, 107
rum, golden
Beach Babe, 71
Caramello Colada, 114

Lychee Crush, 96
Trade Wind, 117
rum, Havana Club 7 year,
in Last Sin, 82
rum, light
Bacardi Classic Cocktail,
45
Bahama Todd, 45
Banana Daiquiri, 71
Bee's Knees, 166
Bella Donna, 92
Black Dog, 45
Blueberry Rocket, 76
Cantaloupe Cup, 100
Chocolate Colada, 163
Chocolate Rum, 163
Daiquiri, 94
El Cerro, 114
Frozen Mango Daiquiri,
98
Gee Whizz, 88
Hibiscus Daiquiri, 171
Honeysuckle Cocktail,
167
Honeysuckle Daiquiri,
167
Kiwi Daiquiri, 90
Love to Love, 178
Mojito, 139
Monte Christo, 97
Naked Lady, 69
Piña Colada, 81
Pome Beach, 120
Pomiri, 121
Sage Love, 142
Velvet Touch, 88

rum, Malibu mango, in
Mango Cosmopolitan, 99
rum, Matusalem, in
Spongecake Martini, 159
rum, 151 proof
Bahama Todd, 45
Chocolate Rum, 163
rum, Parrot Bay, in Baileys
Banana Colada, 164
rum, pineapple-flavored, in
Big Jim Knockout
Punch, 80
rum, spiced
Bahama Todd, 45
Deep Thinker, 134
rum, vanilla
Lavender Mojito, 136
Love to Love, 178

S

saffron, 158
saffron gin. *See* gin, saffron
saffron-infused syrup, in
Saffron Love, 158
sage, 142
Sage Fan, 142
Sage Love, 142
sake, 37, 52–53
Blue Rain, 52
Demon Melon, 100
Hong Kong, 53
Sparkling Sakepom, 53
Wasabi Bliss, 53
salmon, smoked, in Sassy
Salmon, 173

salt. *See also* celery salt
  Classic Tequila Shot, 47
  Russian Experience, 176,
    177
Scotch, 50, 51
  Blood & Sand, 78
  Bobby Burns, 133
  Caveman Crush, 122
  Gillia, 58
  Honey Toddy, 166
  Rusty Nail, 51
Scotch, 12-year-old, in
    Scotch Club, 123
7Up
  Berry Burst, 124
  Elderflower Fizz, 135
sherry, dry
  Alfonso XIII, 189
  Level Martini, 48, 49
  Solero Punch, 107

sloe gin
  Baby Fingers, 116
  Blackthorn, 116
  Brave Love, 116
  Sloe Gin Fizz, 165
soda water, in Acai Punch,
    66
Sourz apple, in Pink
    Flamingo, 106
sparkling water
  Italian White Sangria,
    189
  Mojito, 139
sparkling wine, in Bellini,
    109

spiced rum. *See* rum,
    spiced
spices, 150–159. *See also*
    specific spices
St. Germain elderflower
    liqueur, in Sal's St.
    Germain, 135
strawberries, fresh,
    124–125
  Berry Burst, 124
  Coccinella, 124
  Coco Affair, 80
  Franklin Cobbler, 124
  Strawberry Jive, 125
  Strawberry Margarita,
    125
  Strawberry Spice, 125
  Tropical Butterfly, 125
strawberry liqueur
  Euphoria Cocktail, 132
  Grand Pepper, 156
  Kinky Martini, 159
  Strawberry Margarita, 125
strawberry purée
  Kinky Martini, 159
  Passion-tini, 109
  Possibility, 81
sugar, brown
  Bonito, 107
  Irish Coffee, 82
sugar, demerara
  Deep Thinker, 134
  Pop a Cherry-tini, 79
  Scubarello, 139
sugar, powdered, in Sloe
  Gin Fizz, 165

sugar, superfine (caster)
  Blueberry Caipirinha, 76
  Caipirinha, 94
  Champagne Cocktail, 186
  Coccinella, 124
  French Passion, 108
  Italian White Sangria, 189
  Mint Julep, 138
  Mojito, 139
  Monte Christo, 97
  Pomegrita, 120
  Strawberry Spice, 125
  Tutti Fruitti, 113
sugar cubes
  Old-Fashioned, 51
  Rum in the Old-
    Fashioned Way, 45
sugar syrup. *See also*
    vanilla sugar (syrup)
  Horseradish Margarita,
    182
  Lavenderita, 136
  Lavender Mojito, 136
  Love to Love, 178
  Parisian Smash, 110
sweet chili, in Demon
    Martini, 118, *119*

T

Tabasco sauce
  Bloody Mary, 127
  Vampiro, 127
  Virgin Mary, 127
tangerine juice, in Hot
    Voodoo Love, 182

tarragon, in Tarra Card,
    158
tawny orange, in Tawny
    Orange Jelly Sour, 106
tea, cold, in Coutts, 122
tea, breakfast, in Kentucky
    Derby Cooler, 138
tequila, 37, 46–47
    Bonito, 107
    Brother, 59
    Chinese Lily, 96
    Lavenderita, 136
    Morning Margarita, 87
    Rama, 155
    Stealth Margarita, 153
    Tequila Sunrise, 106
    Tommy's Margarita, 95
tequila, añejo (aged)
    Blackberry Margarita, 72
    Cancun Cooler, 137
    Dark Side, 117
    Fig Supreme, 85
    Hot Gringo, 152
    Mangorita, 99
    Pineapple Margarita, 115
    Tequila Slammer, 47
    Tequil-ini, 47
tequila, gold
    Tequila Shot, 47
    Sangrita Shooter, 47
    Voodoo Breeze, 90–91
tequila, horseradish
    infused, in Horseradish
    Margarita, 182
tequila, reposado, in Sweet
    Indulgence, 85

tequila, silver
    Devil's Butterfly, 84
    Elderflower Margarita,
    135
    Horny Toad, 92
    Margarita, 95
    Rattle and Hum, 178–179
    Rosa Maria, 140
    Strawberry Margarita, 125
    Vampiro, 127

    Watermelon Sombrero,
    128
thyme, 143
    Evening Thyme, 143
    Perfect Thyme, 143
thyme syrup, in Spring
    Thyme, 143
tomato, 126–127
tomato juice
    Bloody Bull, 126

Bloody Mary, 127

Carrot Zest, 180

Sangrita Shooter, 47

Virgin Mary, 127

tonic water, in Maiori
Magic, 60

triple sec

Acai-tini, 66

Evening Thyme, 143

Heebie, 172

Melon Patch, 101

Rhubarb Cosmo, 183

truffles, in Truffle Martini,
173

V

vanilla, in Spongecake
Martini, 159

vanilla rum. *See* rum,
vanilla

vanilla sugar (syrup)

Barbie, 159

Beet-ini, 176

Blueberry Muffin
Martini, 76, 77

Jo Jo Sling, 112

Le Grand Cognac, 187

Limeade, 134

Smoocher, 109

Spongecake Martini,
159

Tarra Card, 158

Vanilla Melon Fizz, 128

vegetables, 174–183. *See
also specific vegetables*

Van Der Hum, in Rattle
and Hum, 178, *179*

vermouth, about, 185, 189

vermouth, dry

Aviator, 189

Basil Martini, 132

Black Dog, 45

Brainstorm, 133

Diamond Dog, 60

Dirty Martini, 102, 103

Friends, 58

Gibson, 42

Kyoto Cocktail, 100

Lychee-tini, 97

Orange-tini, 105

Personality-ini, 102

Rosemary-tini, 140

Rusty Nail, 51

Tequil-ini, 47

Vodka Martini, 49

vermouth, extra dry

Gin Martini, 42

Italian White Sangria, 189

vermouth, red

Bobby Burns, 133

Hong Kong, 52

vermouth, sweet

Americano, 58

Appleton Garden, 67

Aviator, 189

Blackthorn, 116

Blood & Sand, 78

Fifty Casino Cocktail, 117

Hot Voodoo Love, 182

Negroni, 61

vodka, 10, 36, 48–49, 131

Acai-tini, 66

Apple–tini, 67

Apricot Cosmo, 68

Apricot Sour, 68

B B, 70

Beet-ini, 176

Berry Burst, 124

Bitter Kiss, 87

Black Russian, 82, 83

Bloodhound, 59

Bloody Bull, 126

Bloody Mary, 127

Blueberry Muffin
Martini, 76, 77

Campari Nobile, 59

Cape Cod, 84

Carrot Zest, 180

Chocolate Martini, 163

Cinnamon May, 154

Claret Cobbler, 190

Coutts, 122

Cucumber Martini, 181

Deep Passion, 108

Divino, 190

Effen Delicious, 72

Espresso Martini, 82

Evening Thyme, 143

Frescolina, 98

Grand Pepper, 156

Hazelnut-ini, 148, 149

High Heel, 75

Kamikaze Shooter, 94

Lemon Drop, 92

Level Martini, 48, 49

Life Saver, 180

Lychee Lover, 97

Lychee-tini, 97
Maestro, 170
Melon Ball, 101
Melon Patch, 101
Melon-tini, 101
Metropolis II, 187
Monza, 61
Naked New York, 102
Orange Breeze, 105
Oriental Tea Party, 132
Passion-tini, 109
Parisian Blossom, 110, *111*
Personality-ini, 102
Pomegranate Julep, 120
Pome-tini, 121
Rhubarb Cosmo, 183
Russian Experience, 176, *177*
Russian Spring Punch, 75
Saffron Love, 158
Sage Fan, 142
Salty Dog, 86
Sassy Salmon, 173
Screwdriver, 106
Scubarello, 139
Sexy Spring Punch, 73
Smoocher, 109
Strike Out, 121
Truffle Martini, 173
Vanilla Melon Fizz, 128
Va-Va-Voom, 67
Vitamin Hit, 180
Vodka Gimlet, 95
Vodka Martini, 48

Vodka Sour, 93
Wasabi Bliss, 53
Watermelon Martini, 128, *129*
White Cosmopolitan, 84
vodka, apple-flavored, in Scarlet Mischief, 176
vodka, basil
    Basil Martini, 132
    Euphoria Cocktail, 132
vodka, citrus-flavored, in Spring Thyme, 143
vodka, currant-flavored, in Black Door, 74
vodka, Effen, in Rosemary Cooler, 140, 141
vodka, frozen, in Dirty Martini, 102, 103
vodka, honey
    Arabian Dream, 156
    Honey-tini, 167
    Honey, Trust Me!, 167
vodka, horseradish
    Hot Voodoo Love, 182
    Hummer, 182
vodka, lavender-flavored, in Lavender-tini, 136
vodka, lemon
    Dolce Vita, 118
    Lemon Meringue, 93
    Melon Babe, 101
    Zenith, 66
vodka, mandarin
    Choco Kiss, 162
    Metropolis, 105
    Pink Flamingo, 106

vodka, manuka honey, in Chili & Honey Cocktail, 166
vodka, passion fruit, in Pop-a-Cherry-tini, 79
vodka, pear-flavored, 113
    Tutti Fruitti, 113
    Peartini, 113
    Tuscan Pear, 113
vodka, pepper, in Pepper Jack, 156
vodka, raspberry, in Raspberry Collins, 123
vodka, rose
    Heebie, 172
    Rosé-tini, 172
    Spring Pink Martini, 172
vodka, rosemary-infused, in Rosemary-tini, 140
vodka, vanilla
    Big Kiss, 154
    Blueberry Muffin Martini, 76, 77
    Kinky Martini, 159
    Lavender-tini, 136
    Possibility, 81
    Rogue Lemongrass, 137
    Sal's Tart, 86
    Spicy Fifty, 153
vodka, vanilla-infused, in Love, Honor, and Obey, 152
vodka, wild berries, in Wonderful Wild Berries, 121

W

wasabi paste, in Wasabi Bliss, 53

water. *See also* mineral water; sparkling water
Honey Toddy, 166
Mint Julep, 138
Pink Gin, 43
Sweet Indulgence, 85
Tommy's Margarita, 95

watermelon, 128–129
Love, Honor, and Obey, 152
Vanilla Melon Fizz, 128
Watermelon Martini, 128, *129*
Watermelon Sombrero, 128

whipped cream, in Irish Coffee, 82

whiskey, 50–51

white chocolate liqueur
Caribbean Mozart, 162
Chocolate Colada, 163
Chocolate Martini, 163
Luxe Moment, 163

white crème de cacao. *See* crème de cacao, white

white Kina Lillet, in Demon Martini, 118, *119*

white peach purée, in Bellini, 109

white rum. *See* rum, white

white wine. *See* wine, white

wild berries vodka, in Wonderful Wild Berries, 121

wild hibiscus syrup
Hibiscus Daiquiri, 171
Rosé-tini, 172

wine, red
Acai Punch, 66
Claret Cobbler, 190
Code Red, 190
Divino, 190

wine, red (dry), in Red Eye, 191

wine, sparkling, in Bellini, 109

wine, white (dry)
Brazilian Berry, 75
Intrigue, 170
Italian Surprise, 191

wine, white, in Kir, 191

wine flavors, 185–190

Worcestershire sauce
Bloody Bull, 126
Bloody Mary, 127
Carrot Zest, 180
Vampiro, 127
Virgin Mary, 127

acknowledgments

This cocktail book was the result of great teamwork. Thanks to Charles Nurnberg at Sterling Publishing; to my agent, Fiona Lindsay at Limelight Management, and to Lynn Bryan. Many thanks go to Raffaello Dante and Steve McDermott for their assistance with the photographic shoot. Thanks to my son Gerry Calabrese for his support, and a big thank-you to everyone who helped out with inspiration for recipes. To my team at FIFTY, much appreciation for being there. The BookMaker would like to say thanks to Mary Staples for her design; Ian O'Leary for his delicious photographs of the cocktails and the Maestro at work. Thanks to Gemma, too.

We also give grateful thanks to the fruit man, Vincenzo Zaccarini, for his top quality selection of fresh fruit. Marie-Brizard kindly provided the fruit liqueurs.

THE GLASSWARE

We love to show the cocktails in stylish glassware. Following is a list of the glasses used in each photograph: Page 2, Salvatore's Fifty glass; page 5, Ralph Laurent cocktail glass with a Dartington Helen tumbler; page 32, Dartington Scotch whisky glass; page 41, Dartington Exmoor old-fashioned glass; page 49, Baccarat martini glass; page 63, Habitat champagne coupe; page 77, William Yeoward cocktail glass; page 83, Dartington old-fashioned; page 91, Kate Spade tumbler; page 103, Dartington cocktail glass; page 111, Salvatore's own antique flute and cocktail glass; page 119, coupe by IKEA; 129, BookMaker's own from Macy's New York; page 141, Dartington highball; page 147, Dartington Rebecca highball and Charlotte tumbler; page 149, Salvatore's own; page 157, Grip highball design; 176, 179, and 188, BookMaker's own.

SOURCES

www.dartington.co.uk
www.wildhibiscus.com
www.mariebrizard.com
www.pomwonderful.com

about the author

Salvatore Calabrese is an international award-winning expert on cocktails and one of the world's most respected bartenders. He is currently President of the United Kingdom Bartender's Guild. He is holder of the Chevalier du Verre Galant and the Chevalier l'Ordre des Côteaux de Champagne, and Keeper of the Quaiche. His recent awards include 2005 Best New Bar, 2006 Bar of the Year, 2006 Best Cocktail Offering, and Outstanding Achievement Award 2006, and the Italian Bartenders Association (AIBES) awarded him Outstanding Achievement Award 2006. Calabrese is also a world-renowned authority on cognac and vintage cognacs. He is the author of the worldwide bestsellers *Complete Home Bartender's Guide* and *Classic Cocktails*.

www.salvatore-calabrese.co.uk